THE POWER OF
MINDFUL
PARENTING

THE POWER OF
MINDFUL
PARENTING

A GUIDE TO
MORE CONNECTION
AND LESS CONFLICT
WITH YOUR TEEN

WYNN BURKETT

Mindful Parenting Press

To Rita and Chad,
Keep breathing!
Wynn
Burkett

Published by Mindful Parenting Press, San Francisco
www.mindfulparentingofteens.com

Edited and designed by Girl Friday Productions
www.girlfridayproductions.com

Cover design: Kathleen Lynch
Project management: Sara Addicott
Image credits: Cover (and interior fleurons): rustemgurler/iStock; p. 19, 37, 42, 65, 98: Illustrations by Finn Jelinek; p. 28: Gordon Johnson/Pixabay; p. 72: (dancing girl) Streptococcus/Shutterstock, (hearts) Denis Gorelkin/Shutterstock, (confetti) Sudowoodo/Shutterstock

ISBN (paperback): 978-1-7333083-0-4
ISBN (ebook): 978-1-7333083-1-1

Library of Congress Control Number: 2019910389

First edition

Dedicated to my three favorite teenagers:
E, Kat, and Will

CONTENTS

INTRODUCTION

During the mindfulness process, you do not judge, compare, or try to fix your emotions or mind states. Instead you learn to be fully present to whatever you are experiencing, with a calm, nonjudgmental mind and an open heart.

—*Phillip Moffitt,* Emotional Chaos to Clarity

Welcome, mindful parent! Yes, I mean you. Chances are that if you picked up this book, you're already the mindful parent of a tween or teen. You're no doubt doing your best to raise your child or children with wisdom and good intentions. And yet, despite the fact that you're a thoughtful, caring parent, you're still the recipient of a disturbing amount of adolescent eye-rolling and attitude. It's perplexing to realize that your sweet, loving child has been body-snatched by a surly teenager. You may be asking yourself if it's ever going to be fun again, while wondering if you'll even survive the next several years.

It will be, and you will. I promise. But first you'll need some mindful parenting tools at the ready.

Seven years ago, my business partner, Ann Arora, and I developed a workshop called How to Tame Your Teen by Taming Yourself First: A Mindfulness-Based Approach to Parenting, which we've been teaching in schools and in our communities around the San Francisco Bay Area ever since. The idea for the class came from our own challenges as parents of teenagers. Ann is a professional psychotherapist with a successful clinical practice in San Francisco where she treats adults who struggle with depression, anxiety, and post-traumatic stress, and I'm an executive coach and leadership consultant with close to twenty years under my belt working with professionals to create happier, more productive, more meaningful lives and business cultures. We're highly trained in the field of emotional intelligence, and yet all too often, we found ourselves reacting to our teens in ways that brought out the worst in us (and in our families).

It became clear to us then that raising adolescents required a trip back to the parenting drawing board. Tweens and teens pose a particular challenge for all parents: when our children were younger, we could exert some influence over them, but as they grow up, we have a lot less control over their actions and reactions. In fact, though we might sometimes wish otherwise, in this phase of parenthood all we really have control over is ourselves. What Ann and I came to see, and what inspired our workshops, was that when *we* could be less reactive and more emotionally centered with our teens, we had a positive impact on our relationships with them and the health of our whole families.

Our personal parenting difficulties inspired a deeper dive into what we each had been doing in other parts of our lives, just not consistently applying (yet) to our mothering. Ann and

I had both meditated for years, and in our professional practices, we shared mindfulness skills and tools with our patients and clients. We wondered if we might adapt some of these mindfulness practices to help us deal with our kids better. As we started to deliberately bring mindfulness skills to our parenting, we both quickly saw that they worked—not always, not perfectly, but when we could be calmer and less reactive with our teens, they were calmer and less reactive with us. This led to the creation of a curriculum that we now share with other parents facing the same struggles.

Over the many years that we've taught this class, parents show up for a variety of reasons. Most come wanting to understand this new landscape of parenting teenagers. Often what has worked for them in the past isn't effective anymore. They want less conflict and more connection during this difficult phase. They want to know when to step in and when to step back. They're looking for ways to stay calm when their buttons are being pushed. They want to be more present, avoid saying hurtful things, and repeat themselves less. They want to help their teens stay safe while encouraging growth and allowing for those all-important mistakes. They want less distress and more warmhearted moments. Many want their households to be calmer and more fun. When it comes down to it, they want to parent with compassion and kindness and to create and maintain relationships with their kids for the long term. When they leave the workshops, many say they feel like they have the tools to reach these goals—now they just need to remember to use them and be intentional in how they parent.

But not everyone can come to our workshops, so I wanted to write a book to help more parents feel empowered to make changes in their relationships with their teens and hopefully create more joyful, peaceful homes. In our classes we've tried to avoid abstract concepts about mindfulness, and I've tried to do the same in the pages of this book. Here I offer mindfulness and meditative exercises and techniques that are concrete and directly related to parenting teens. This book is meant to be experiential. There are questions to ponder, skills to try, and meditations to practice. No background in Buddhism or meditation is required, just a willingness to explore some powerful new tools at your disposal.

So why mindfulness? Mindfulness helps us stay present, patient, and openhearted during these intense teenage years. As a parent of a teen, you will inevitably deal with situations and feelings that are unanticipated and unpleasant. Mindfulness doesn't change what's going on with our teens, but it can change how we are with them. Mindfulness helps us stay calm and tap into our instinctive wisdom, compassion, and resourcefulness.

This book is written to help mindful parents like you navigate the tricky adolescent years. As parents ourselves and through our work with our parent communities, we've seen the benefits of these tools and practices firsthand. We're not perfect parents—not by a long shot. We've each had our bumps in the road and made our share of mistakes. This book is not about controlling your teen; it's about staying calmer and controlling *your* reactivity to your teen. Mindful parenting can help you have less conflict and more moments of love and connection in your family.

CHAPTER 1

The Challenge of Adolescence: Why Parenting a Teen Is So Hard

The dawn of puberty is a stormy period of great agitation when the very worst and best impulses in the human soul struggle against each other for its possession.

—*G. Stanley Hall,* Adolescence, 1904

PONDER THIS

List five words or phrases that describe how you're parenting your teen.

1. _____
2. _____
3. _____
4. _____
5. _____

Now list five words or phrases that describe how you want to parent your teen.

1. _____
2. _____
3. _____
4. _____
5. _____

As psychologist G. Stanley Hall observed in 1904, teenagers have been vexing to adults for a long time. And even if today we better understand the physical and psychological changes of adolescence, it doesn't make living with our children any less frustrating than it was a century ago. On one hand, they're still completely dependent on us, and on the other, they're doing everything in their power to drive us away. This duality can be extremely difficult to navigate gracefully, and it's often compounded by the loneliness of doing so without a lot of support. Unlike in the baby and toddler years—where parent groups, extended family support, and mommy-and-me classes might have been more readily available—we often face the teen years alone. Some of this isolation is self-imposed. Many of us are more reluctant now to share what's really going on in our families, because the ways our teens act can feel demeaning and dismissive, if not downright dangerous. And most of us worry that their offensive behavior is a reflection of us as parents. Plus, as our kids get older, we're less likely to talk about the struggles we face because the stakes are higher. We don't want our kids' teachers or other parents to know that our teens are engaging in defiant, risky, or even illegal behaviors. Probably more than at any other stage, we as parents doubt ourselves and may feel judged by others—ironically, at the same time that our kids are feeling more judged too. This perception isolates us exactly at a point when we should be coming together as adults and sharing thoughts, emotions, and strategies for dealing with teens.

The transition from childhood to adulthood is a dramatic one, and for teenagers today, the stressors and expectations are unprecedented. The ever-present access to and influence of social media, which feeds insecurity and creates pressure to present a perfect life, coupled with demanding academic expectations (and the ever-more-competitive college-application process), can leave our kids feeling overwhelmed and inadequate. In the past ten years, rates of anxiety and clinical depression among teens have reached an all-time high. In fact, in 2017 the National Institute of Mental Health estimated that 3.2 million adolescents (13.3 percent of the US population aged twelve to seventeen) had had at least one major depressive episode in the previous year.[1]

But there's no need for despair—parenting mindfully can help you navigate these challenges with more optimism, compassion, and courage.

ADOLESCENCE: WHAT IS GOING ON?!

One of the main tasks of adolescence is to achieve an identity—not necessarily a knowledge of who we are, but a clarification of the range of what we might become, a set of self-references by which we can make sense of our responses, and justify our decisions and goals.

—*Terri Apter,* Altered Loves

We all want love and harmony in our homes, but the reality is that conflict becomes a bigger part of our family dynamics as our children move into the tween and teen years. There are reasons for this, which are largely developmental, so let's spend a little time talking about teen psychology and development.

Baby Self / Mature Self

It's useful to start with the construct of the baby self and the mature self, as described by psychologist Anthony Wolf in his exceptional book on parenting teenagers, *I'd Listen to My Parents If They'd Just Shut Up*.[2] As Wolf describes it, every human being has both of these aspects to their personality. Children naturally exhibit the baby self more readily, while adults typically display their mature self most of the time. Teens fall somewhere in the middle and can shift back and forth between the baby self and the mature self over the course of a day, an hour, or a conversation. The baby self is the part of us that wants to be cared for, nurtured, and coddled. It's the part of us that doesn't want to perform or fulfill any responsibilities. The mature self is the responsible part of us that meets expectations, follows social norms, and has empathy for others.

Think about how these two parts of your own psyche play out in the day-to-day. When a friend reaches out and asks for a favor, your mature self readily agrees to help because you genuinely desire to be useful to your friend. Alternatively, imagine arriving home after a long day of work and flopping onto the sofa for some well-deserved R & R, only to have your partner ask if you wouldn't mind getting up and helping unload the groceries from the car. The mature self knows you should just fulfill this simple request. And yet your baby self feels resentful and resistant. Not because you don't care for your partner or don't want to do things for them, but because, in the moment, having to get up from the couch seems like an unbelievable imposition. In other words, a simple request becomes an outsized one in your "baby mind," and thus the response is disproportionate. Ring any bells?

Your teen experiences the same thing, only more so. Imagine for a moment what a typical teenager's day is like. They spend most of their time putting on their mature face. They get themselves out of bed (when they really need more sleep) and off to school, switching gears several times a day as they move from classroom to classroom, subject to subject, and teacher to teacher (each with their own styles and expectations). Maybe the teen has an after-school job, sport, or other extracurricular activity to boot. They must navigate all this, every day, in addition to dealing with the crushing social pressures of being a teenager. In other words, they are required to present their mature self for much of the day.

No wonder when they get home, their baby self shows up in full force. If we adults feel exhausted after a day of being on our best behavior, think how teens must feel. They have a lot less practice at it than we do. And at some level, your teen understands that with you, they can be the worst-possible version of themselves and you'll still love them. They will use this unspoken knowledge to test your boundaries (and your patience). And because they're secure in your unwavering support, they will often be their baby self—just like the adult in our example could be with their caring and devoted partner who just wanted a little help with the groceries.

Seen in the right light, this behavior is actually a compliment and affirmation of your good parenting. Your kids trust that they can be their worst and know (at a subconscious level) that you'll still love them (even if you might not like them very much in the moment). And rest assured that they actually do know how to behave, evidenced by how they can be intolerable at home and yet perfectly polite and socially adroit with friends, other parents, teachers, and coaches. How many of us have had the experience of hearing from another adult how delightful our teen is and wondering if they could actually be talking about our child?

In fact, even if your relationship with your tween or teen doesn't feel all that positive, a 2004 study of five thousand adolescents found that over 80 percent of teens think highly of their parents, and over 75 percent enjoy spending time with them.[3] Though you may be convinced that your child lands clearly in the 20 percent who don't think well of their parents, the odds are in your favor. The facts are that teenagers generally respect, admire, and like their parents (they just don't let us know it).

The Goal Is Autonomy

In addition to the baby-self behaviors you may be seeing in your adolescent, there are profound psychological factors at play. Between the ages of twelve and twenty-two, humans go through several developmental stages to reach the ultimate milestone of autonomy. Autonomy is the state where we are separate from yet emotionally connected to our parents. By the end of college, most children are healthily separated from their caregivers. They've developed a sense of their own individual identity and a sensitivity to and respect for others. In fact, this healthy ability to separate while staying connected is foundational for their future relationships.

Separation

In order to achieve this desirable state of autonomy, an adolescent's primary developmental task is to form an identity. To do this, they move through two sequential and predictable stages.[4] The first is called *separation*. Separation starts around age eleven or twelve and is roughly aligned with the middle-school years. This is when a child's biology drives them to realize that they are different from their parents. Unsurprisingly, this stage is marked by distancing behavior. For girls this often takes the form of becoming more combative with Mom and Dad, and for boys it often takes the form of withdrawing. But as with many gender-based generalizations, these behavioral differences are highly variable; if you happen to have a girl who withdraws or a boy who's combative, that's perfectly normal. Whatever form separation takes, tweens will (unconsciously) choose the strategy that provides the most distance from us.

The separation stage is also characterized by significant physical changes, which contribute to the insecurity and awkwardness that go hand in hand with adolescence. As with other developmental stages, it's a matter not of *if*, but *when*. Most kids go through these physical changes over a span of five years or so, with the greatest variation apparent in the middle-school years. Just think about what a class of kids in this age group looks like. There are those (especially girls) who start developing as early as ten or eleven, while others may not begin puberty for another three to four years. These dramatic bodily changes can be unnerving for kids, because, preoccupied as they are with body image, they're painfully aware of where they fall on the developmental spectrum. By high school, these differences even out more, at least when it comes to the major physical changes of puberty; but during the separation phase, adolescents are constantly comparing themselves to their peers and are often miserable about how they measure up. Unfortunately, there's not much we can do about this except be compassionate about the fact that their changing bodies are probably causing them a lot of shame and embarrassment. Knowing this, if they do happen to express their worries to us, we can set an intention to listen empathetically and take their concerns seriously.

Another characteristic of the separation phase is an obsession with friendships. Adolescents care deeply about their relationships with their peers and look to them for approval, connection, and a sense of identity and belonging. This is an important part of their beginning to psychologically differentiate from their parents—but to us, it can feel like a painful and jarring rejection. Seemingly overnight, they go from caring about and wanting to please us to caring about and wanting to please their friends. This can be especially true with adolescent girls, whose climbing estrogen levels trigger their brains to talk more, interact with their peers more, think about romantic relationships more, and emote more.[5] It's important to know and remind ourselves that this behavior is all part of normal adolescent development and not a rejection of us or the result of something we've done wrong as parents.

This is also a time when adolescents may develop a strong desire for privacy. If you're a parent who likes to keep tabs on what your child is doing, know that these efforts will suddenly be perceived as intrusive and unnecessary. Unlike the younger child who came home from school and enjoyed a snack and a friendly chat about their day, a tween or teen will most likely head right to their room and pointedly shut the door. The desire to be left alone can be amplified in boys due to increasing levels of testosterone at puberty, which causes decreased interest in talking and socializing.[6] Again, this feels personal, but it's not. Pushing us away is part of the necessary process of separation that allows them to become independent young adults. To be clear, I'm not saying that you should stop interacting with or checking up on your kids during this phase; in fact, you absolutely should continue to do so—just don't expect them to like it.

Individuation

After separation, adolescents move through the next developmental phase: *individuation*. This phase usually starts around age fourteen or fifteen and roughly aligns with the high-school years. Kids in this phase are psychologically asking themselves, "If I'm not who I was when I was a child, and I'm not my parents—which I know I'm not, because I don't even *like* my parents—then who am I?" Their biology is driving them to answer this important question of identity, one that helps shape them into healthy adults. The individuation stage is marked by significant cognitive development, continued conflict, and ongoing efforts to create distance from us.

Cognitively, teenagers develop rapidly during the high-school years, becoming increasingly capable of complex thought and reasoning. This is, in part, why they can suddenly run circles around us in an argument. As they seek more independence, they can also think more abstractly and question different points of view, leading to more confrontation and conflict. Again, looking at it in the right light, you can take pride in your teen's ability to think with growing complexity and creativity. These emerging cognitive skills facilitate the transition from dependency to autonomy.

Still, in the moment, this process of individuation, coupled with the teen's newfound rhetorical prowess, can be annoying and exhausting. Add to the mix that this is a time of increased risk-taking, which is psychologically necessary for forming identity. Teenagers are seeking new sensations and experiences, including risky ones, to help form who they will become. Some of this may take the shape of experimenting with alcohol, drugs, sex, and other consequential, potentially risky behaviors. A teen's brain chemistry increases the drive for reward, at a time when they aren't always well equipped to anticipate consequences or weigh the risks before trying something new.[7]

To address these potential risks, it helps to understand what's going on with adolescents regarding alcohol, drugs, and sex, so parents can provide guidance and set limits for our kids. As much as we might prefer to hide our heads in the sand, the reality is that even "good" kids engage in these behaviors. According to a 2018 study funded by the National Institute on Drug Abuse, 59 percent (the majority) of eighteen-year-olds reported that they had consumed alcohol, while 24 percent had done so by eighth grade.[8] And although teenage use of marijuana and other illicit drugs has held steady from 2013 to 2017, there's been a notable increase in vaping, that same report shows.[9] With regard to sexual activity, a study by the Guttmacher Institute revealed that 40 percent of surveyed high-school students in the US had had sex. While just 20 percent of ninth graders studied had had sex, a full 57 percent of twelfth graders had done so, reflecting the fact that as they get older, teens are more likely to become sexually active.[10]

These statistics are provided not to alarm you, but to arm you. Thinking through these potentially high-risk situations ahead of time and educating yourself about them helps you address them more constructively when they come up. Each family can clarify their values, establish rules regarding these behaviors, and engage their teens in (short, information-based, ongoing) conversations about them. A 2018 study showed that parents *can* influence their teen's behavior by monitoring their activities and helping them think through these issues ahead of time so they make better decisions when faced with these situations in the real world.[11]

Also, don't be surprised if, in the spirit of experimentation, your teen changes friend groups at least once during high school or drops an activity they've done for years to try something different. All of a sudden, your avid soccer player may decide they hate the game and want to join the drama club. This is all normal and necessary experimentation in their quest to understand who they are. It's important for parents to know what's driving these changes and to set boundaries around unsafe risks while encouraging their kids to take safe, appropriate risks. That's often easier said than done; it requires ongoing attention to and connection with your teen at a time when you might feel frustrated with or disconnected from them.

Part of what makes the separation and individuation phases so difficult for parents is that these phases are proceeded by a developmental stage called *latency*. Latency occurs from about age five to age ten or eleven and is the least psychologically conflicted period in a human life. Latency is often a pleasant time, when children are developing new capabilities, friendships, and interests. During latency, children are likely to be agreeable and eager to please. The contrast from this easier latency phase to the more difficult adolescent phase can be stark and therefore upsetting for parents.

The bottom line is that, despite how the change feels when it's happening, it's not personal. The processes of separation and individuation are inevitable and necessary to reach autonomy, which is a healthy, desirable state. (Nobody wants their kids living in their basement at age thirty!) And yet this constant state of pulling away, even though it's natural and necessary, is a major source of conflict between parents and teens.

THE TEEN BRAIN

Dramatic psychological changes are not the only transformations afoot in these adolescent years. There are also significant shifts happening in the structure and function of the teenage brain. Over the past twenty years there has been an explosion of research about the human brain, largely due to advances in scanning technology. As a result, we now know a lot more about how our brains develop and function.

Notably, it takes much longer than was once thought for the human brain to mature. Experts used to believe that the human brain was fully developed by the age of eight years old. We now know that the brain is not fully grown until the age of twenty-five (on average), or well into young adulthood.[12] A fully developed brain is defined as one where neural pathways are "wired together" to relay signals, which is how information is processed. Although this integration process speeds up in adolescence, the teen brain is "under construction" as this happens. Since their brains are still a work in progress, teenagers are unable to process information as efficiently as adults.

The last part of the human brain to mature is the prefrontal cortex, which functions as the CEO or governor of the brain. It is responsible for executive functions such as planning, judgment, reasoning, impulse control, organization, understanding consequences of behavior, and the parental favorite, *prospective memory*: the ability to remember something you agreed to do in the future, like turning in your completed homework in class tomorrow rather than leaving it crumpled up at the bottom of your backpack.[13] Teenage brain development is uneven: some parts of the adolescent brain are developed while other parts are still evolving. The prefrontal lobes are significantly underdeveloped in teenagers compared to adults, which explains some of your adolescent's unpredictable behavior. For example, most teenagers have well-developed cognitive abilities yet are significantly more impulsive and reactive than adults. That can be confusing and frustrating for parents. How can they ace calculus and yet consistently forget to close the refrigerator door? It's important to know that teen behavior is driven in large part by a brain that's not yet fully integrated. This understanding will help you stay mindful. It's easier to remain calm when you realize that you're dealing with a problem that is not wholly of the other person's making.

The human brain is also largely shaped by our experiences. The toddler years are the only other period in the human life span when the brain changes as rapidly and goes through as much rewiring as it does in the teen years. As the teen brain is restructuring, the teen's experiences during this period will impact how their neurons "wire together" and create lasting neural pathways, leading to enduring patterns and habits. It's vital that we parents stay connected with our teens and engaged in their lives during these important years (even if our influence is unwanted), so we can gently guide our kids toward positive experiences and role models, and away from negative ones, while the brain is still forming.

The more teens know about what's happening in their brains, the better. Approaching conversations about risky behavior by leading with brain science might be a more effective tactic than focusing only on right and wrong.

The Amygdala and the Prefrontal Cortex: An Unlikely Pair

Another vital bit of brain science to understand is the relationship between the prefrontal cortex and the amygdala. The human brain is a complex organ made up of many interconnected parts and processes. For our purposes, I've simplified things and focused on two regions that play a key role in explaining some of the behavior you're likely to see in your teenager: the amygdala and the prefrontal cortex (PFC). What happens in the teenage brain is much more complicated than just how these two regions interact, but their interplay does explain some elements of teen behavior. Put simply, the amygdala is the *reactive* part of the brain, and the prefrontal cortex is the *reflective* part of the brain.

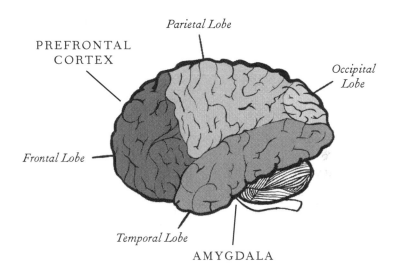

The amygdala, an almond-shaped structure at the base of the brain, is part of the limbic system—a set of neural structures that deal with emotion and memory. The amygdala is responsible for some of our most basic functions, such as breathing and blinking, as well as controlling our reflexes and processing emotions (like anger and fear). The amygdala is sometimes referred to as *the primitive brain*; it was one of the first parts of the brain to develop in the human species and is responsible for the most fundamental processes. The amygdala is responsible for the fight-or-flight response—part of its job is to be constantly vigilant, scanning the environment for potential threats. Because it was important to the survival of the species for humans to avoid life-threatening experiences, our brains have evolved with a negativity bias: we detect negative events more quickly and remember negative events more read-ily.[14] When the amygdala perceives a danger, it reacts reflex-ively to protect us. This reaction can have a positive result, such as when we stumble and our brain signals our arms to shoot out and stop ourselves before we've even registered that we've fallen. Sometimes "acting before thinking" is beneficial and keeps us safe.[15] We can thank the amygdala for that.

Another part of the brain that's relevant is the prefron-tal cortex, which is responsible for executive functioning and higher-order thinking. Located behind the forehead, the PFC is the last part of the brain to develop (remember, it's not fully mature until the midtwenties) and helps govern our thoughts, feelings, and behaviors. Our PFC helps us make sound deci-sions, consider consequences, control impulses, reflect, think abstractly, organize, contribute to moral decision-making, and plan ahead. It allows us to make sense of the information that's coming into our brain and react appropriately. It's the part of our brain that puts the brakes on an emotional reaction and helps us respond more wisely. In contrast to the amygdala, the PFC performs the vital function of *stopping* us from acting before thinking.

It's important to discuss these two areas of the brain because we live in a modern world of complicated social inter-actions, with a brain created millions of years ago to keep us safe in a world of physical dangers. To accomplish this, the amygdala is designed to override the PFC when we feel anxious, fearful, or threatened. Recall a time when you reacted impul-sively and lashed out without thinking. You probably said or did something you later regretted. Rather than responding in a rational way, in that moment your amygdala took over and your prefrontal cortex went offline.[16] Daniel Goleman, who writes about emotional intelligence, describes this phenomenon as an "amygdala hijacking."[17] An amygdala hijacking occurs when the PFC is flooded by stress hormones, and we're unable to control our emotions or manage our response. When this happens, we literally *aren't thinking*. After an amygdala hijacking, we can reflect back on our behavior and feel regret for having acted illogically or inappropriately, but at the time we had little control over our reaction.

While the amygdala is well developed at birth, the PFC is the last part of the brain to mature. Teens feel anger and fear more often and more intensely because their amygdala is more active than that of a child or an adult, while at the same time, they don't have a fully developed PFC to consistently govern their emotional responses.[18] This effect is magnified when teens are stressed or tired.[19] Have you ever asked your teen, in your nicest voice, "Sweetheart, could you please bring your plate from the table to the sink?" only to have them shriek, "Why are you always yelling at me?!" That's the amygdala talking. In that moment, your teen feels angry or threatened, and their amygdala triggers a secretion of hormones that overwhelms their rational brain. If this scene is familiar to you, you've had firsthand experience of your teen reacting reflexively to a perceived insult without thinking logically.

It's useful to understand a little about how your teen's brain develops, for a number of reasons. First, it explains behavior that appears impulsive and overly dramatic. Your teen simply isn't thinking straight (or able to control themselves) when they're flooded. Second, it can be reassuring to know that an amygdala hijacking is partly a function of an undeveloped prefrontal cortex, and as this part of the teen's brain develops, these reactions will decrease. Rather than getting angry or annoyed at them, you can observe your teen's behavior with curiosity and try not to take their irrational, explosive behavior personally. And finally, and maybe most important, you as a parent can make sure that your teen's outsized reaction doesn't trigger an outsized reaction in you. You don't want your amygdala to also get hijacked so your reaction matches your teen's. In the moment, if you can notice that your teen's amygdala is flooded, you can step back, consult your own more highly developed prefrontal cortex, and make the choice to dampen rather than fuel the fire.

It's useful to note that since a teenager's prefrontal lobes are not completely mature, sometimes we adults can play the role of a *surrogate* prefrontal cortex. Since they are still learning how to make decisions, plan ahead, and express emotions in a grown-up way, we can model good executive functioning. For instance, we can ask them questions to help them think through issues, understand consequences, and reflect before acting. Questions like "What are the steps you might take to get the project done by the due date in two weeks?" or "That comment you made may have come across in a hurtful way. How do you think that made your friend feel?"

Another helpful tactic is to share with your teen what's going on in their brain during adolescence. It's enlightening for them to know how the amygdala and prefrontal cortex interact, so that some of their own dysregulated behavior is more understandable to them. Also, knowing about neuroplasticity (how the brain changes with experience) and how neural pathways are being laid down during this period of rapid growth can help your teen understand the importance of creating good habits and adopting a "growth mindset."

In Stanford psychologist Carol Dweck's book *Mindset: The New Psychology of Success*, she explains the importance of how we think about our intelligence, talent, and abilities.[20] If you believe that you have only a certain amount of intelligence, talent, and ability (a fixed mindset), then you are likely to believe that you have to prove yourself over and over again to confirm these qualities. In contrast, if you believe that these characteristics can be developed and grown with concerted effort (a growth mindset), then you will view your experiences as opportunities to learn. It's the difference between looking at failure as a judgment on your abilities versus seeing it as a chance to assess where you went wrong so you can adapt and learn. Dweck explains that traits like an aptitude for math or an ability to write well aren't fixed; because of brain plasticity, these skills can grow and develop with practice and attention. Teens should know that intelligence and talent are not fixed characteristics, but can be cultivated through dedication and hard work—throughout our lifetimes, but especially during this period of explosive neural growth.

Understanding some of the psychological and cognitive development of the tween and teen years gives us a clearer insight into what's going on with our kids and hopefully more compassion for their impulsive, often irritating behavior. This knowledge can also help us remember to not take their behavior personally, helping *us* be less reactive in the moment.

CLOSING

In light of the significant developmental changes your teen is experiencing, how would you like to react the next time they have an amygdala hijacking or show a lack of executive functioning?

_____
_____
_____
_____
_____
_____
_____

CHAPTER 2

The Role of Mindfulness in Parenting Teens

Mindfulness means paying attention in a particular way: on purpose, in the present moment, and nonjudgmentally.

—*Jon Kabat-Zinn,* Wherever You Go, There You
Are: Mindfulness Meditation in Everyday Life

PONDER THIS

Do you have a meditative practice? If so, how has it helped you in your life and as the parent of a teen? If you don't have a practice and would like to, what have been obstacles to starting one?

_____

_____

_____

_____

_____

_____

_____

_____

_____

_____

_____

_____

_____

CALMNESS IS CONTAGIOUS

Mindfulness is transformative, because it can fundamentally change the way a person sees the world and copes with stress. As we start feeling more emotionally centered from our meditative practices, other people feel it when they're with us. Calmness is contagious—if one person is calm, everyone around them stays calmer. And really, that is the crux of this book. If you as a parent can tap into that calmness when dealing with your often highly reactive teenager, not only will *you* benefit because you'll feel in control and effective as a parent, but *your teen* will feel calmer too. This effect will lead to less conflict and more moments of love and connection. Isn't that what we all want?

So how do we get there? Let's start with a little background on meditation.

Whether you are new to mindfulness or a seasoned practitioner, you'll benefit from understanding its origins. It all started with the Buddha, who was born a prince in India around the sixth century BC. His given name was Siddhartha Gautama, and he led a privileged, sheltered existence until the day he decided to leave his palace and explore the world beyond. In his journeys he encountered the realities of sickness, old age, and death. He was so shocked and distressed by what he saw that he gave up his wealth and position and committed himself to understanding human suffering and how to end it. After years of spiritual seeking, he finally decided to simply sit under a tree and meditate until it all made sense. One night, under a clear, brilliant sky, the Buddha achieved enlightenment. The resulting Four Noble Truths summarize his realizations:

1. Suffering is an inescapable part of life.
2. The cause of suffering is our attachment to needs and desires.
3. We can end suffering by letting go of our attachments.
4. The Eightfold Path (illustrated below) helps us let go of attachments and achieve freedom from suffering.

The Buddha spent the rest of his life in India teaching the Four Noble Truths as the path to enlightenment. Eventually Buddhism spread to many other parts of the world, including Tibet, China, Southeast Asia, and Japan. Each time it reached a different country, the philosophy transformed and emphasized different practices. Buddhism started to take root in Europe and the United States in the mid-twentieth century, as Westerners who studied and trained in Thailand, Burma, and India brought this practice home. And recently a new form of Buddhism has emerged, often referred to as Vipassana, or insight meditation. A secular manifestation of Buddhism, Vipassana does not teach a system of religious beliefs, but rather focuses on techniques that allow us to see clearly into our own natures, showing us how to use this wisdom to interact with the world more adeptly. The mindfulness skills you will learn in this book are based on teachings from insight meditation, coaching, and other therapeutic modalities.

CONQUERING MONKEY MIND

Quite simply, mindfulness is the practice of being fully aware in the moment. Jon Kabat-Zinn, one of the leading pioneers of mindfulness in the United States, defines it in his book *Wherever You Go, There You Are* as an awareness that arises from "paying attention in a particular way: on purpose, in the present moment, and nonjudgmentally."[1] We create this awareness when we bring our attention to the present moment intentionally, without judgment—being present with our experiences, our interactions, and, most important, with ourselves and our inner lives.

Why is mindfulness important? Much of life's suffering stems from ignorance or lack of understanding about ourselves and our nature, which causes us to make unwise choices. Mindfulness increases *insight* because it draws our attention inward, trains our minds to be fully present to our experiences, and enables us to observe our inner emotional processes. As our insight about ourselves and the world around us grows, so does our wisdom.

Most of us spend the vast majority of our time in a state that practitioners refer to as "monkey mind," where our thoughts are jumping from one thing to the next like monkeys swinging from tree to tree in the jungle. The monkey mind worries about the future and ruminates on the past, continually distracted by one thought, judgment, or emotion after another. Most of us are reacting constantly to this flurry in our minds, which results in stress, depression, and reactivity. Mindfulness enables us to go beneath the surface of moment-to-moment life and recognize that our thoughts and feelings are fleeting and do not have to define us. This ability to observe our inner process creates some distance from the chatter, reducing its power over us.

Let's look at how mindfulness might manifest in our parenting lives:

A Not-So-Mindful Approach

It's Wednesday morning, and your teenager hasn't emptied the garbage, although this job is part of his regular chores. Frustrated about his ignoring your requests, you blow your top, yelling at him. He yells back at you and calls you some nasty names before he stomps off to school. Begrudgingly, you take the garbage out again. This ruins your day, and you can't stop thinking about it. You feel angry about his dismissive attitude, guilty because you lost your temper, and sad because you can't figure out how it all went wrong. You can't stop replaying the scene in your head.

A More Mindful Approach

You notice that your teen has not taken the garbage out again, and you feel the anger building in your chest and throat. You notice the chain reaction of thoughts and judgments that come from this emotional state and how they seem to fuel your anger even more. You also notice how bad this makes you feel. You shift your attention away from the narrative

*in your head, moving it to your body and breath. You
take a couple of deep breaths and let your attention
linger there for a moment or two. You begin to notice
that your emotions are diminishing; the tightness in
your chest and the pressure in your throat are less-
ening. You contemplate saying something to your
son about the garbage, but because he's stressed and
you're both running late, you decide not to address it
in the moment. You also choose not to take the garbage out for your son, deciding instead to address the
issue after he returns from school. You don't get stuck
in a bad mood the rest of the day because you were
able to maintain a healthy distance from the experience and stay in control.*

The first example represents a pretty typical parent-teen
interaction. We've all been there. Angry feelings lead to yelling
and name-calling, and we feel miserable because it happened
again. Both the parent and teen are highly reactive, which
leads to conflict. The parent has a hard time letting go of what
happened, and her monkey mind takes over and tortures her
the rest of the day.

In the second example, things unfold differently. The parent is connected to her body. She can feel the anger rise up in
her chest and throat, yet it doesn't overwhelm her. She's able
to observe her thoughts and judgments and see how they are
fueling her anger. That power of observation creates insight
into what's happening in the moment and helps her maintain
some distance from her emotions. When we can observe and
name our emotions, it helps us not overidentify with them,
so they are not all-consuming. When we have a more mindful approach, we start to see the teen behaviors that regularly

cause us to react emotionally and can rehearse our responses ahead of time so we act in calmer, more purposeful ways.

Importantly, the parent in the second example took a breath. Most of us hold our breaths when we feel stress, which reduces the amount of oxygen going to our brains. When you pause and breathe, more oxygen enters your bloodstream, which helps regulate your nervous system. This focus on her breath enabled that second parent to stay calm and center herself before she made any decisions about how to respond. Because she was able to slow down her reaction, she chose not to address the issue right away. Sometimes pausing when you feel triggered is the wisest thing to do. She decided not to enable her son's forgetfulness by doing the chore for him, and to deal with the issue later when she had more distance from the experience. Last, the incident didn't bother her for the rest of the day, because she didn't react instantly and could control her emotional response.

Sound impossible? It's not, and the information in this book can help you more consistently tap into your natural wisdom and equanimity. A more mindful approach includes planning ahead for those recurring events that we know set us off. Over the next several chapters, you'll learn skills to help you observe how your thoughts and judgments drive your behavior toward your teen. You'll also learn a lot about your emotional experience as a parent, what triggers you, and how to disengage from unnecessary conflict. Those skills, along with a few others, will help you feel calmer in general and more effective as a parent. But you can't do any of this without learning and practicing the most important skill of all: meditation.

MEDITATION AS PART OF MINDFULNESS?

Meditation is the foundation of any mindfulness practice. Think of it as the road map to a mindful existence—you can't get there without it. Meditation requires us to sit quietly with ourselves and focus our attention on one thing for an extended period of time. Researchers have found that with only thirty hours of a mindfulness-based stress reduction practice, meditation changes the wiring in our brain associated with stress and reactivity.[2] The more time we spend meditating, the more easily we can remain calm, focused, and skillful in the conduct of our day-to-day lives. Although the benefits of meditation get stronger the more total hours you practice,[3] don't let that daunt you. Even meditating for a few minutes at a time can reduce your reactivity and help you feel calmer.

Meditation teaches us to focus the mind, at least temporarily. Many people believe that successful meditation means emptying the mind and entering a blissed-out state. While it is possible to access various states of consciousness while meditating, the goal isn't to empty the mind of thought. Rather, meditation calls us to focus the mind on one thing—maybe the breath, a body part, or a sound. This sustained focus quiets the endless mental chatter and allows the mind to *relax*. The relaxed state brings many benefits, including a reduction in stress. Our nervous systems, especially the part responsible for processing stress and the fight-or-flight response we discussed in chapter 1, have evolved to keep us safe from dangerous predators. It's basically a feedback loop that takes in a stressor in the form of information and pushes it up to the brain for processing. If the brain deems it to be threatening, the body reacts instinctively in ways that aim to keep us alive.

When the stressor goes away, the body returns to the relaxed state called *equilibrium*.

Although some stress is useful and in fact critical to our survival (remember the fight-or-flight response of the amygdala?), most of us rarely encounter life-or-death situations; rather, we deal with chronic stress, the kind that never really goes away. A high-pressure job, a difficult teenager, a fractured marriage—none of these is likely to kill us, but they all cause tension and have health consequences nonetheless. When we experience chronic stress all the time, our bodies never get back to a healthy equilibrium, a state of rest.[4] That constant tension is linked to many diseases, including hypertension, heart disease, anxiety, depression, and obesity.[5] This is where meditation and mindfulness can help. When we meditate consistently and direct our attention to the present moment, *it brings us back to equilibrium.* It allows our bodies and our minds to rest for a bit, which reduces stress and fortifies us to move forward and manage the challenges in our lives.

Consistent meditation also trains our minds to be more present. It helps us tame monkey mind. Most of us spend the majority of our time ruminating on the past or worrying about the future, which causes anxiety and depression because we can't change or affect what's already happened or know what might happen. Meditation trains our minds to be present with our experiences, good and bad. It helps us learn to tolerate different emotional states and observe their natural cycle. Knowing that emotions ebb and flow can make them easier to tolerate and process.

Meditation also helps us stay open to the joy and wonder of the present moment by engaging our senses. Sadly, many of us go through our days without noticing and experiencing all the wonderful things around us—a beautiful sky or a friendly smile. The more time we spend training our minds to be present, the more we can accept and enjoy what life brings us each day.

Consistent meditation also helps us build awareness about our inner experiences. Meditation draws our attention inward and trains our minds to observe our inner dialogue without judgment: what triggers us, how we feel, how our bodies feel, how we react when we feel that way, and so on. This ability to observe is very important, because it helps us build insight into our emotional experiences while simultaneously creating a bit of distance from them. Insight and distance are helpful when choosing how to respond in heightened or challenging situations.

All the benefits associated with a consistent meditation practice—including decreased stress, improved cardiovascular health, a stronger immune system, better mood, and improved psychological functions like attention, compassion, and empathy—will help you be a more mindful parent. Meditation is like building a muscle: the more you exercise it, the stronger it gets and the more quickly the benefits generalize to your daily life. Feeling calmer and less stressed will enable you to be less reactive when interacting with your teen. Staying in the moment will help you connect more meaningfully and consistently with your kids. And feeling more emotionally centered will help you respond more effectively to your teen's own emotions. What's more, your calmer state will have a contagious effect on those around you, including your kids. All it takes is the cultivation of a regular practice.

MEDITATION IN PRACTICE

Meditation is the noble act of making friends with yourself. Breath by breath, moment by moment, you begin to learn who you really are. At first, this prospect may seem interesting, shocking, appalling, mysterious, or boring. Eventually, though, as you practice meditation, your mental chatter starts to quiet, and you find natural attunement with yourself.

—Susan Piver, Quiet Mind: A Beginner's Guide to Meditation

There are many types of meditation—sitting, walking, standing, lying down—but the most common form is the sitting meditation. The idea is to use your body posture to support your practice, so the first step is to get comfortable. Start by finding a quiet place where you can sit comfortably with a straight spine. Sit in a way that allows you to be both relaxed and alert. If you're seated on a cushion on the floor, put your bottom slightly higher than your legs, which you can cross loosely in front of you. If you're in a chair, sit squarely on the seat, with both feet flat on the floor and your bottom against the back of the chair. This elongates your spine, which helps you stay alert. In either case, rest your hands comfortably in your lap.

You can close your eyes or keep them open by lowering your gaze and focusing on a fixed point in front of you. Try dropping your attention into your body and really noticing the sensation of your feet on the floor and your bottom on the chair or cushion.

Once you have settled your body, start by paying attention to your breath. Breathing is so natural to us that we're barely conscious of it—which makes it an excellent focal point. Resting your attention on each inhale and exhale, simply noticing, accepting, and being aware of your breath, helps focus your attention and brings you into the present moment. When you attend to the breath itself, you allow thoughts and feelings to come and go without getting caught up in them. The thoughts will arise, you'll notice them, and then you'll return your attention to your breathing. Thoughts are like waves rolling up on a beach—they roll in, then they roll out. Your goal is not to stop them, just to not follow them out to sea.

In addition to helping you focus your attention, deep breathing calms your body. Breathing deeply activates your parasympathetic nervous system (PNS), which triggers your body's relaxation response. The PNS is responsible for keeping your body in a steady state. It quiets the body and the mind so you feel relaxed. In order to activate the PNS, you can practice something called *diaphragmatic breathing*—or belly breathing. The diaphragm is the muscle located beneath your ribs. If you place your hand there and watch it as you breathe, you'll see your hand rise and fall with the inhale and exhale. If you exaggerate your breathing so the rise and fall of your hand is more obvious, this will activate your body's PNS and reduce anxiety. Another simple way to stimulate the PNS is to inhale as deeply as you can, hold the breath for several seconds, then gradually let the air out while relaxing your body.[6]

Throughout this book you'll find a variety of meditations that support each chapter's topic. You can read and familiarize yourself with each meditation, or you can visit https://mindfulparentingofteens.com/mindful-meditations/ to find an audio recording that will guide you through the meditation.

The first meditation to try is the Mindful Breathing Meditation.

MINDFUL BREATHING MEDITATION

To begin, find a comfortable position for your body and allow yourself to relax.

Take three long slow deep breaths, in through the nose and out through the mouth. As you breathe slowly and deeply, see if you can make your exhale as long or longer than your inhale. This triggers your body's relaxation response and will help you feel calmer.

Return your breathing to its normal pace and notice the ease and effortlessness of your breathing. Observe the constancy and consistency of your breath. Bring your attention to those parts of your body where you feel your breath most. Tune in to each breath and notice the sensations that are present as you breathe in and out: the coolness in your nostrils, the expansion in your chest, or the gentle rise and fall of your belly. Remember, there's no right or wrong way to experience your breath. Just let your attention rest on your breath as it gently goes in and out. There's no need to control your breathing in any way, just allow your body to breathe itself.

As you're paying attention to your breathing, you may notice that your mind wanders. When this happens, simply acknowledge that this is what our minds do. It's not a problem or a mistake. Simply notice and acknowledge that this is what the practice is about: seeing the patterns that remove us from the present moment. This wandering of attention, noticing the wandering, and gently returning the attention back to the present is the practice. Take a few moments in silence to continue resting your focus on your breathing.

As this meditation comes to a close, remember that your breath is always available to you as a resource. If you feel anxious or distracted, your breath can help ground you in the here and now and anchor you in the present moment.

When you feel ready, open your eyes and return your attention to the room.

If you would rather listen to a guided meditation, please visit https://mindfulparentingofteens.com/mindful-meditations/.

What was that Mindful Breathing Meditation like for you?

_____

_____

_____

_____

_____

_____

_____

_____

_____

_____

_____

_____

_____

_____

_____

_____

_____

_____

_____

_____

_____

_____

_____

_____

_____

_____

_____

_____

Not everyone will have the same experience when meditating, and that's okay. Many people find the initial experience of breathing mindfully to be surprisingly easy and relaxing. In a short time, they are able to follow their breath, drop into their bodies, and calm their minds. Others find it challenging to pay such focused attention to their breathing. In fact, they might even feel like they can't breathe, which is _anything_ but calming. If this is the case, don't worry—you're not doing anything wrong. The act of paying attention to something we normally do without a thought can feel strange and uncomfortable. Try again at another time and see what happens as you become more familiar with the experience. And know that any meditation is beneficial, because it strengthens your ability to focus your attention.

If you find that it's hard to remain present, you're not alone. Many people find it difficult, especially in the beginning. It's also important to remember that recognizing that you're not present and your mind is wandering takes a certain amount of mindful awareness. Mindfulness is a practice and a process. And like anything, the more you do it, the better you become at it; building the meditation "muscle" is no different.

The diagram below illustrates what happens to our attention when we meditate. Typically, we start our meditation by focusing our attention on something like our breath, then our mind begins to wander. At some point we become aware that our mind has wandered, and we consciously and intentionally refocus on the present moment. That whole process—not just the part when we're actually present—is mindfulness. So the next time you're meditating and you notice that your mind got distracted, instead of beating yourself up, gently note where your mind went and bring it back to the moment.[7] *This is the practice!*

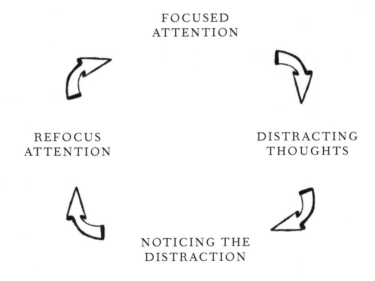

FOCUSED
ATTENTION

REFOCUS   DISTRACTING
ATTENTION   THOUGHTS

NOTICING THE
DISTRACTION

CLOSING

Did you try meditating or some other mindfulness practice? If so, describe the experience and how it has impacted or might impact your interactions with your teen.

_____

_____

_____

_____

_____

_____

_____

_____

_____

_____

_____

_____

_____

_____

_____

_____

_____

_____

_____

_____

_____

CHAPTER 3

The Power of Thought: Observing to Create More Effective Behavior

Our life is shaped by our mind: we become what we think. Suffering follows an evil thought as the wheels of a cart follow the oxen that draw it. Joy follows a pure thought like a shadow that never leaves.

—Buddha *(from* The Dhammapada, *translated by Eknath Easwaran)*

PONDER THIS

What qualities are you most proud of as a parent?

_____

_____

_____

_____

_____

_____

_____

What qualities are you least proud of as a parent?

_____

_____

_____

_____

_____

_____

Although parenting a teen is often hard, know that a lot of what you're doing is already working. It's important to appreciate the qualities you possess that contribute to your parenting well. Knowing what these characteristics are helps you set intentions for yourself and how you want to be with your children. When you are parenting mindfully, you are more present, purposeful, and able to embody more of these traits. And although you might also have some qualities that you're not so proud of, there's no need criticize yourself for them. Instead, let them guide you toward where your mindfulness practice can go.

MINDFUL THOUGHTS

When you meditate, do not try to have good thoughts, do not try to keep away bad thoughts, do not try to stop thoughts, and do not try to go after them. Rather, rest in the state of being aware of thoughts as they arise.

—*Kalu Rinpoche,* Gently Whispered: Oral Teachings by the Very Venerable Kalu Rinpoche

Part of being mindful is training ourselves to be friendly observers of our internal processes. Thinking is habitual and powerful. We human beings spend countless hours in thought, which is why "monkey mind" is such an apt description. When we start paying attention, we become aware that we are frequently engaged in one activity while having thoughts about something else. By observing these thoughts more consciously, we see that they are relentless and often repetitive. In fact, you may notice that the thoughts you have today are the same thoughts you had yesterday and will likely have tomorrow. Mindfulness helps us pay attention to what we're thinking in the moment rather than letting our thoughts run on autopilot.

To be clear, thoughts, even these "monkey mind" thoughts, are not bad. In fact, they're often necessary for us to thrive. Thinking allow us to communicate, solve problems, motivate ourselves, and inspire others. But it can also drive us to misinterpret events, create fear and anxiety, and actually prevent us from thriving. When we pay attention mindfully, we see our thoughts for what they really are—plans, opinions, or judgments—and realize that they may not reflect what's actually going on in the moment. Sometimes our experience is based more on what we *think* than what we actually *see*.

Mindfulness helps us realize that we are separate from our thoughts and that our thoughts don't always reflect reality. When we start noticing that we're having a thought and are able to observe it in the present moment without necessarily believing it or acting on it, then we start to experience the benefits of nonjudgmental awareness. The aim isn't to stop having thoughts, but to learn to notice them as they're happening and develop a wise relationship with them, knowing that thoughts are real, but not necessarily true. And whether true or not, we don't have to act on each and every one.

HOW INTERPRETATIONS DRIVE REACTIONS

Most people don't realize that the mind constantly chatters. And yet, that chatter winds up being the force that drives us much of the day, in terms of what we do, what we react to, and how we feel.

—*Jon Kabat-Zinn, interviewed in* Healing and the Mind, *Bill Moyers*

What we say and do with our teenagers is a function of how we think and feel about them. If we can learn to separate the facts from our interpretation or judgment of the facts, we can gain insight into our own reactions to our teens. With this insight, we can be more intentional about our responses and behave in ways that are more skillful. Mindfulness helps us bring kind, nonjudgmental attention to our thoughts. And by observing our thoughts, judgments, and emotions in a curious, open-hearted way, we can bring more compassion and composure toward our teens (and ourselves).

Let's go through the exercise below using a simple, real-life example of how thoughts impact behavior. I'll use the all-too-common example of a messy teen bedroom.

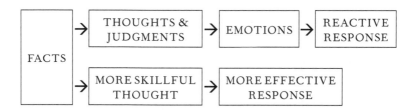

We start with the **facts**. A fact is something that is observable and indisputable, and that anyone can agree on, like "It's 70 degrees today." In the messy-room scenario, the facts might include:

- There are dirty clothes and worn athletic gear scattered on the floor.
- There are unwashed plates and half-full mugs of tea (with the tea bags still in them!) on the desk, bookshelf, and bedside table.
- There are damp towels on the hardwood floors (which were just refinished last month).
- The laundry basket of *clean* clothes has been sitting in the middle of the room for three days now.
- You have asked your teenager every day (sometimes even more) for the last week to clean the room.

Does this scenario sound familiar? After establishing the facts, the next step is to look at your own thoughts, judgments, and interpretations about these facts. For instance, in the "70 degrees" example, your interpretation might be "It's warm out today" or maybe "It's a little cooler than I like" or possibly "This is perfect weather." In the messy-room scenario, the thoughts, judgments, and interpretations are likely to be more complicated and charged. They might include:

- My daughter is such a slob.
- My teenager is a spoiled, entitled brat.
- How can someone *think* in a room like this? No wonder her grades have slipped.
- My son disrespects me and the rules of our household.
- He'll never have roommates at college because no one would want to live with this mess.

- We give our teen nice things and he just trashes them.
- If she cared about me, she'd do as I ask.
- Someone this lazy will never hold down a job.
- I must have done something wrong to have raised such an irresponsible child.

You get the idea. When confronted by the messy room, our thoughts and judgments get activated immediately, and we quickly find ourselves having an emotional reaction. In our "70 degrees" example, the way we interpret the fact that it's 70 degrees will drive our emotions. Whether we feel happy or disappointed or bored, those feelings result from our *interpretation* of this fact. Similarly, our emotions about the messy room are driven by our assessment of the facts. We might feel any number of emotions about the messy room, including:

- Anger
- Sadness
- Frustration
- Rage
- Disappointment
- Resentment
- Defeat
- Guilt
- Fear

Once we've identified the thoughts and emotions that the messy room brings up for us, the next thing to do is to look at how these thoughts and emotions influence how we react. What is our automatic, reactive response to a room that's *still messy* after a week of asking that it be picked up? Maybe we yell something nasty or hurtful at our teen. Perhaps we go in and clean the room ourselves (while muttering profanities under our breath). Or maybe we lose it and ground our teen for a month.

We've all been there. Voices raise, doors slam, tempers flare. The problem is that these reactions aren't constructive. They rarely produce the outcome we want—or if they do, it's emotionally costly to ourselves, our teenager, and our relationship. These encounters usually leave us feeling drained and disheartened.

So what's the alternative? We suggest practicing **more skillful thoughts** and brainstorming **more effective responses**. A more skillful thought is one that integrates your knowledge about teenage development and shifts your perspective, so you can replace your habitual negative interpretations of your teen's actions with ones that lead to more judicious responses. You can use these thoughts to remind yourself that this isn't a permanent state of affairs, you can handle this, and you can be the adult and stay calm. A skillful thought might emphasize that this situation is temporary and that you are strong enough in the moment not to let it get under your skin.

Some more skillful thoughts about the messy room might be:

- All teenagers are like this.
- I can handle this.
- My daughter is going through a messy phase.
- Her prefrontal cortex isn't fully developed, so her organizational skills aren't fully developed.
- My son works hard; he can leave his room in whatever state he wants.
- I'm going to be the adult here and not get angry right now.
- This won't make any difference in ten years.
- I'll bring this up later when we can talk about it calmly.

- My son is doing the best he can, and I'm doing the best I can.

These more skillful thoughts lead to more effective responses. They help you tolerate distressing situations and encourage you to stay calm in the moment so you can problem-solve more helpfully. For instance, instead of screaming and threatening your teen with a lifelong grounding, you might instead just *close the door* so you don't have to look at his messy room. Or you might decide to revisit your family policy on housekeeping and choose to have a conversation with your teenager about this at a later time. Or maybe you create a rule and consequence, such as: the room has to be cleaned every Thursday in order for your daughter to go out on the weekend. The suggestion isn't that you stop setting boundaries or guidelines, but instead that *in the moment*, you choose a more effective response. Then you can revisit the situation and explain what's expected when both you and your teen are calmer. That way, there's a greater likelihood that your teen will be able to hear the request and—hopefully—comply with it.

Working through this exercise can help you get ahead of recurring conflicts. You can probably easily identify a handful of situations in your family that repeatedly cause discord between you and your teen. Not being ready for school in the morning, not returning your texts or calls when they're out with friends, not abiding by a curfew, or overusing electronic devices all might fall into this category. Use the chart below to think through these trigger situations ahead of time, so that when they occur you can keep your cool and act in wiser, more productive, more compassionate ways. The goal is to decrease conflict in the moment and stay connected with your teenager as you set expectations and establish boundaries.

Here's what the messy-room scenario might look like if you mapped it out:

FACTS

- Dirty clothes on floor
- Unwashed plates on desk, bookshelf, bedside table
- Damp towels on floor
- Laundry basket of clean clothes unpacked
- Repeatedly asked for room to be cleaned

THOUGHTS / JUDGMENTS

- My daughter is a slob.
- My teen is a spoiled brat.
- How can you think in this room?
- My son disrespects me.
- No one will ever want to be roommates with him.
- He trashes his stuff.
- If she cared, she'd do as I ask.
- She'll never hold a job.
- I must have done something wrong.

MORE SKILLFUL THOUGHTS

- All teens are like this.
- I can handle this.
- Her prefrontal cortex isn't fully developed.
- He can leave his room however he wants.
- I'm not going to get angry right now.
- This won't make any difference in ten years.
- I'll bring this up later when we can discuss calmly.
- My son is doing the best he can, and so am I.

EMOTIONS

- Anger
- Sadness
- Frustration
- Rage
- Disappointment
- Resentment
- Defeat
- Guilt
- Fear

MORE EFFECTIVE RESPONSE

- Close the door
- Revisit housekeeping policy
- Room must be cleaned every Thursday if teen wants to go out on weekend

REACTIVE RESPONSE

- Yell at my teen
- Clean room myself
- Ground teen for a month

Exercise: Pick a trigger situation in your family and work through the chart below.

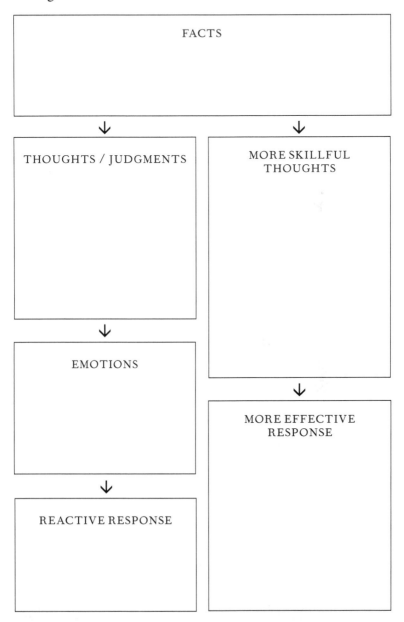

FACTS

↓ ↓

THOUGHTS / JUDGMENTS   MORE SKILLFUL THOUGHTS

↓

EMOTIONS

↓

MORE EFFECTIVE RESPONSE

↓

REACTIVE RESPONSE

REFLECTION

What are you learning about how your thoughts, judgments, and emotions impact your behavior toward your teen?

_____

_____

_____

_____

_____

_____

_____

_____

_____

_____

In the last chapter we explored the Mindful Breathing Meditation; the second foundational meditation is the Body Scan. The Body Scan Meditation helps you be more aware of your body and release stress and tension, allowing yourself to rest and relax. The focus is on the sensory experience of being in your body, which helps free you from your thoughts and emotions and puts you in a more grounded, calmer, present state.

BODY SCAN MEDITATION

Start this Body Scan Meditation by getting comfortable in your seat. Roll your shoulders forward several times, then reverse the circles and roll your shoulders back in the opposite direction. Tilt your neck to the right, stretching out any tightness or tension, then tilt your neck to the left. Now slowly twist your upper body to the right side, and then twist your upper body to the left side. Allow your torso and back to unwind and relax. Close your eyes and gently rest your hands in your lap. Bring your awareness to your whole body and imagine any tightness or discomfort melting away. Now focus on your breath, breathing in calming energy and breathing out stress and tension.

As you become more relaxed, focus on your body as a whole. Notice how you're sitting. Notice the feeling of the air as it touches your skin. Feel the weight of your body in your seat and the sensation of your feet planted solidly on the ground.

Bring your attention to the top of your head, your skull, your scalp, and then to the sides of your head, your ears, and your face. Notice any tightness you might be holding in your face—your forehead, your brow, the muscles around your eyes, your jaw—and gently release any tension there. Feel your muscles unclench and loosen as you gently relax.

Now bring your attention down to your neck and shoulders. Gently scan them and notice what sensations are there. There may be parts of your body where you don't feel any sensations; that's okay, you don't have to try to create sensations—you're just noticing what's there and what's not there. If there's tightness or pain, you can breathe your loving attention into these areas and let the discomfort go.

Observe the sensations you feel in your arms and hands. Move your focus from your upper arms to your lower arms to your fingers and thumbs. What do you notice? Do you feel tightness, discomfort, tingling? Whatever is there, just let it be and bring your healing attention to those areas.

Scan down to the middle of your body. Notice your chest, your abdomen, your back. This is where many of your vital organs live. Gently scan and see what is present. Notice the gentle rhythm of your heart, the easy in and out of your breath, and the gurgling sounds and sensations in your stomach. Now bring your attention to your hips and pelvic region. What do you sense in your left hip, your right hip, and the pelvis itself? Breathe into these areas and relax even more. Now scan down to your thighs, your knees, your shins and calves. Notice any sensations there. Are they pleasant, unpleasant, or neutral? Observe whatever is there with friendly curiosity. Now bring your focus down to your ankles and the tops of your feet, the soles of your feet, and your toes. Pay attention to any sensations, breathe into them, and let go completely.

We'll end the body scan bringing your attention back to your body as a whole. Notice how each part of your body is connected to another. What does presence feel like in your body? Observe the weight of your body in your seat. Feel your feet firmly planted on the floor. Feel your skin as it touches the air around you.

> *Take one last deep breath, and when you're ready, open your eyes and bring your attention back to the room.*

If you would rather listen to a guided meditation, please visit https://mindfulparentingofteens.com/mindful-meditations/.

What was that Body Scan Meditation like for you?

_____

_____

_____

_____

_____

_____

_____

_____

_____

_____

_____

_____

Like your breath, your body is always available to you, serving as an anchor to the here and now. When you're feeling triggered or reactive, you can drop your attention into your body, observe the sensations that exist, and ground yourself in the present moment. This focus on the body can help you relax and shift your attention from unhelpful thoughts and emotions to the direct sensory experience of how it is to be inside your own skin.

CLOSING

What are you learning about how your thoughts and judgments impact your behavior toward your teen?

_____

_____

_____

_____

_____

_____

_____

_____

_____

_____

_____

_____

CHAPTER 4

The Power of Emotions: Noticing to Reduce Reactivity and Stay Calm

Feelings come and go like clouds in a windy sky. Conscious breathing is my anchor.

—*Thich Nhat Hanh,* Present Moment Wonderful Moment: Mindfulness Verses for Daily Living

PONDER THIS

What would be different about your home if there were less arguing with your tween or teen?

_____

_____

_____

_____

_____

_____

_____

_____

_____

_____

_____

_____

_____

_____

_____

MINDFUL EMOTIONS

Just as mindfulness meditation helps us bring attention to our breath, body, and thoughts, it also trains us to look at our emotions with loving awareness. Our emotions often run our lives. When events trigger us, we typically react in habitual ways without consciously choosing how we want to respond. And emotional overwhelm can affect our ability to think and reason. Our emotional state can determine our actions—so the more familiar we are with our emotions, the more choice we have about how we act and the less likely we are to be mindlessly driven by them. Understanding our emotional triggers can help us respond more graciously toward our teens.

So what is an emotion? An emotion starts as a complex physiological reaction in your body. You sense something in your environment through electrical and chemical signals in your body. These signals start as information you take in through your senses; the information is communicated through your nervous system to your brain, where it's processed in the limbic system. The limbic system, connected to other parts of the brain and body, signals your response. An emotional experience will produce automatic, unconscious changes in the body. You might feel these changes in any number of ways, including tension in the muscles, fluctuations in heart rate, or changes in skin temperature.

Emotions are real and important to pay attention to. They signal that something in your environment is impacting you. Once an emotion is triggered, you can't stop the reaction in your body. The better you get at noticing your bodily sensations, the better you'll be able to choose how you respond to the information coming in and manage your reactions in a more intentional way. Do you notice yourself clenching your jaw, hunching your shoulders, or feeling something in the pit of your stomach?

What signals do you get when you're starting to feel an emotion? Here's an exercise to help you practice noticing the sensations in your body that accompany your emotions.

EXERCISE:
NOTICING EMOTIONS

Sit in silence for a moment or two. With your eyes closed, recall some recent interaction with your teen that was upsetting to you, one where your teen really pushed your buttons. Maybe you felt disrespected or had an argument with them that was particularly upsetting. Picture what happened as vividly as you can, as if you were reporting it for a newspaper. Now identify exactly what you're feeling. Think of some words that describe the emotions you're experiencing. Be as precise as you can. Do you feel angry, frustrated, scared, confused, or ashamed? Give the feelings a name. Come up with a word or words that epitomize the painful experience.

Now let your attention wander to your body. Become aware of the physical sensations that arise as you locate the emotion you've identified. Find the sensations the memory brings up. For many, it's pressure in the chest or a sensation of tightness in the gut. Some feel pressure in the throat. Find where it is in your body and hold that emotional experience for several moments. When you're ready, open your eyes and answer the questions below.

DESCRIBE YOUR EMOTION

Name the emotion: _____

Draw a picture of where you sense the emotions in your body:

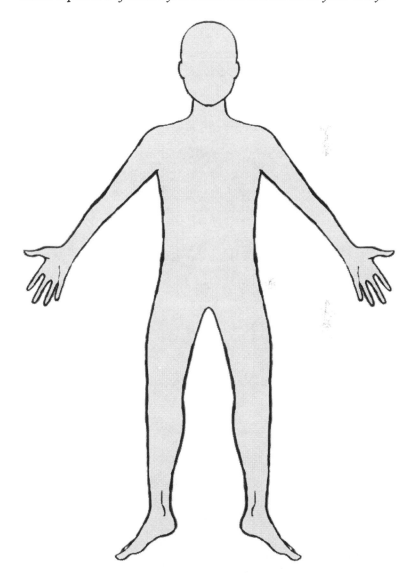

Describe the sensations that go with this emotion.

_____

_____

_____

_____

_____

_____

_____

_____

_____

Describe common triggers for this emotion.

_____

_____

_____

_____

_____

_____

_____

_____

Describe the thoughts and judgments that accompany this emotion.

_____

_____

_____

_____

_____

_____

_____

_____

How does this emotion drive how you react toward your teen?

_____

_____

_____

_____

_____

_____

_____

How would you like to respond toward your teen in this situation?

_____

_____

_____

_____

_____

_____

An example might look like this:

> *You were aware that your teen had a big project due in his history class. For the last few weeks, you casually asked about it—trying not to nag but to make sure the work got done—and your son assured you the project was on track. Yesterday, you opened your email to find a message from his teacher telling you that your son didn't turn in the project and currently has a D+ in the class. When your son got home from school, you asked him about it and he seemed unconcerned. You noticed an immediate surge of energy in your body. It started in your chest and quickly came up through your throat. Your heart beat faster, you*

*felt shaky, and your cheeks flushed. You identified
many emotions that you were experiencing, including
anger, upset, worry, and disappointment. These emotions drove you to accuse him of being irresponsible,
lazy, and disrespectful. Even thinking about it now
gives you an upset stomach.*

This exercise shows you how to practice becoming more
familiar with your emotions: how to feel them in your body,
notice how they cause you to react, and observe how they drive
your attitudes and behaviors toward your teen. When our
teens trigger us, it's easy to react without thinking, in ways that
are not mindful or effective. As you become better at noticing
the sensations in your body that are associated with your emotions, you can use this information to pause and respond more
adeptly.

COMMONLY FELT EMOTIONS

Feelings can be complex and overwhelming. An important part
of any mindfulness practice is to get comfortable with noticing
and then naming our emotions. By doing this, we develop a
greater understanding of, and perspective on, our emotions.
Once we've noticed that we're experiencing an emotion, naming it creates distance so we can feel it without getting caught
up in it. A 2006 study at UCLA by Matthew Lieberman and
colleagues showed that the mental labeling of an emotion triggered activity in the prefrontal cortex and reduced activity in
the amygdala, which diminished the subjects' emotional reactivity.[1] Through mindfulness we can start to look at our emotions more objectively and say to ourselves, "Oh, this is what
worry feels like" or "That is anger" or "There's judging here."

The list below includes some common emotions. Copy the list and post it on the fridge or your bathroom mirror to help you become more keenly aware of the array of emotional experiences you might have on any given day.

Right now, I feel . . .

Adored	Fragile	Proud
Amazed	Frightened	Regretful
Angry	Frustrated	Relieved
Annoyed	Furious	Resentful
Anxious	Grieving	Respected
Apologetic	Guilty	Restless
Ashamed	Happy	Sad
Bitter	Hopeful	Satisfied
Blessed	Horrified	Scared
Bored	Hurt	Scattered
Cautious	Inadequate	Secure
Cheerful	Indifferent	Self-conscious
Comfortable	Insecure	Shocked
Confident	Interested	Shy
Confused	Irritated	Silly
Content	Jealous	Sorry
Delighted	Joyful	Strong
Depressed	Judging	Stupid
Determined	Lively	Surprised
Disappointed	Lonely	Suspicious
Disturbed	Loved	Tense
Eager	Mad	Tired
Embarrassed	Miserable	Uncomfortable
Empty	Motivated	Vivacious
Energetic	Nervous	Vulnerable
Enlightened	Obsessed	Worried
Envious	Overwhelmed	Worthless
Excited	Peaceful	Worthy
Foolish	Pleased	

The more we're able to observe our emotions with curiosity, simply accepting them without trying to change them, the better we can see the range of emotions that pass through our hearts and minds, and not be identified with each and every one. As thirteenth-century poet Rumi observed in the poem "The Guest House" (found in full at the end of this chapter), rather than resisting emotions, we can invite them in and "treat each guest honorably." The point isn't to stop feeling, but to be a better observer of our feelings so we can decide how we want to respond to them. When we sit quietly and see the coming and going of our emotions, we notice that they are constantly changing and that we can choose how, when, and whether we'll act on them.

NOTICING THE SECOND DART

One side effect of really noticing our emotions is that we can start to see how emotions build on each other; often, when triggered, we find ourselves having "feelings about our feelings." Noted author and psychologist Rick Hanson writes how the Buddha called this reactive, unconscious cascade of emotions "the second dart." Buddha observed that physical and emotional pain, as well as pleasure, are an inevitable part of life. Experiencing a painful event is "the first dart." The second dart is our reaction to the first one. It's the one we sling at ourselves when we negatively judge how we responded to the first painful dart.[2]

For example, your teen says something rude that provokes an emotional reaction in you. You feel it as a surge of energy in your chest and throat. You interpret this physical sensation as anger. Recognizing that you're angry, you might then feel ashamed for getting mad, or sad that you feel rejected by your teen (the second dart). Ironically, we can also have a negative reaction (second dart) to a positive event. For example, when something good happens to us, we feel the pleasure of it, then might quickly experience guilt about it or worry that we don't deserve this good thing. Noticing and acknowledging the second dart with openness and curiosity is the first step toward reducing the reactivity. If you can stay present to the first dart, then you see what's there without reacting further, and thus can begin to reduce the chain of suffering.

DISENGAGEMENT STRATEGIES

As you get better at noticing the sensations in your body, which serve as an early-warning system that an emotional reaction is happening, you can use this information to inform how you interact in the moment with your teen. What we teach in our workshops is what Anthony Wolf refers to as the art of "disengaging."[3] We're not advising that you disengage from your teen, but instead that you disengage from the argument that's about to happen. Unless it's a safety issue, it's usually not effective to respond immediately when you're triggered, especially if you're angry. Responding angrily usually makes a bad situation worse. Teenagers often don't back down and, most of the time, will match our anger or exceed it. It's more skillful to disengage from the escalation in the moment. This doesn't mean that you don't address the situation with firm limits and consequences, but it's often wiser to do so when emotions have cooled down and equilibrium has been reestablished.

So how do you disengage from your teen's unreasonable behavior, resistance to your requests, or escalating emotions? Try calling on one or more of these four methods:

Pause and Breathe: When you feel triggered, a simple pause and a deep, slow breath can prevent you from saying something in reaction to your teen that you might later regret. Recall that by pausing and breathing, you bring more oxygen to your brain, lower your heart rate, and calm your nervous system. Most of us are conditioned to respond immediately, so when we instead deliberately pause and breathe, we create a momentary delay, giving us time to make a more purposeful choice about how we want to respond. This is especially useful with charged topics. You can buy yourself time by using language like "I'm not ready to talk about that right now" or "I need time to think about this."

It can also be helpful to pause and breathe before you reply to a text or email. Here's a real-life example: One morning before my teenage daughter left for school, I asked her to do two simple tasks during the day. At lunchtime, she sent me a text saying, "I did the first thing." My initial reaction, which I wrote in the text box, was "What about the second thing? Did you do that?" Luckily, before I pushed "Send," I paused for a moment, thought about how my response might be received, and changed the message to "Great, thank you! 🏃 ❤️ 🎉 ." Right away, I got a text back from my daughter: 💙 💙 💗 . Rather than an immediate, reactive response from me, the more mindful text created a moment of connection between us. (And if you're wondering, she did in fact do the second task later that day.)

Talk Less: When our teens start arguing with us, our natural instinct is to argue back. We jump into the discussion so we can convince them of the rightness of our position. This almost never results in the desired outcome, because our teens will argue with us with excruciating persistence. In this case, *talking less* can help you disengage. We recommend using the "broken record" communication technique in which you repeat your answer as often as needed, in the simplest, fewest words possible.[4] It's best if you can use a bored, neutral tone so as to not escalate the argument. It might sound like this: "I'm sorry the answer is no . . . I hear you, and the answer is no . . . Nevertheless, the answer is still no . . . The answer is no . . . No." The goal is to stick to the mission (you're not allowing a particular thing to happen) rather than being triggered by your teen's insolent attitude or sidetracked by their irrelevant arguments like "You're the worst mom in the world . . . This is so unfair . . . You're ruining my life . . ." and so on.

Stop Talking: If the escalation continues despite your best efforts, there may come a time at which the most skillful way to disengage is to stop talking completely. You've already made your point, and continuing to repeat yourself isn't going to advance your cause. It's helpful to tell your teen what you're doing so they don't interpret your disengagement as hostile or withholding. You can say something like "I think we've said enough right now. I'm going to stop talking now." The challenge of the "stop talking" strategy is that you actually have to *stop talking.* This can be exceedingly hard when you have so much to say on the topic. The best way to stop talking is to distract yourself from the argument by using your mindful techniques—such as taking deep, deliberate belly breaths; dropping your attention into your body; or busying yourself with some distracting task like washing the dishes.

One of the consequences of not talking is that you allow your teen to have the last word. You've already done your job as a parent by saying no or enforcing a consequence. An argument is basically a power struggle, and your teen knows that ultimately you have the power. By letting them have the last word, you might allow them to save a little face in the relationship.

The other consequence is that they hear themselves speaking and have to live with the weight of their words. In contrast, if you continue arguing with them, they make you the bad guy—and in their mind, that lets them off the hook for anything horrible that they've said. Your children know what's acceptable to say and what's not. If the last words they hurl at you are "I hate you" or "You're such an idiot," then they have to sit with the discomfort created by the nasty comment that just came out of their mouth. Sometimes, after an exchange like this, they will come back later and apologize. If you keep arguing with them, they won't take any responsibility for the exchange, nor will they feel inclined to acknowledge any regret they might feel for what they said.

Walk Away: The final disengagement strategy is to *walk away*. As with the other strategies, you don't want to do this in a volatile, combative way, like slamming the door as you exit the room or racing off in your car with the tires screeching. Instead you want to do it mindfully and calmly, by telling your teen that you're leaving the room to take care of yourself. By saying something like "I'm going to walk away now, because I need to go clear my head," you reduce the risk of them feeling abandoned. Again, it's not that you're disengaging from your teen, but that, in the moment, you disengage from the *conflict* with your teen. It's not only appropriate but often necessary to circle back later when emotions aren't running so high, to finish the conversation and make sure your rules and expectations are clear.

The practice is to recognize your emotions as they arise without judging them, so that you become more and more familiar with your own internal experience. Although we practice meditations "on the cushion," the true test is when we're caught in the throes of an argument. Can we notice then that we're being triggered, not get rattled, and act with wisdom and skill to disengage from a brewing conflict?

TAKING CARE OF YOURSELF

If you are gentle with yourself you will become gentle with others.

—*Lama Thubten Yeshe, "Bodhicitta: The Perfection of Dharma"*

It's critical to take good care of *yourself* during these tumultuous teen years. Having a regular self-care routine is important because it builds stamina and resilience. Resilience is the ability to bounce back from adversity or stress and find your way back to equilibrium. Part of resilience is accessing the resources you need to sustain your well-being. Making sure you have a healthy diet, regular sleep and exercise, and plenty of opportunities to be outside in nature and to connect with people you care about are very beneficial to your physical and emotional health. And an attention to self-care also sets a good example for your teen; nobody wants to raise children who don't know how to take care of themselves.

Self-care includes actively practicing compassion toward yourself. Most of us find it easy to express compassion when a friend or family member is going through a difficult time, but it's a lot harder to find compassion for ourselves. What if we turned our innate desire to ease others' suffering and support their happiness toward ourselves? When you are compassionate with yourself, you treat yourself gently and notice when you're being self-critical or judgmental of yourself. When you witness yourself doing this, you can choose to change your response. Instead you can begin to view yourself with kindness, act as a supportive friend to yourself, and remember all the times you did the right thing for your child. Mindfulness is the key to self-compassion: rather than avoiding or problem-solving when you're feeling upset, you can stop, become present, and face the truth that you're going through a hard time. Once you've acknowledged this, you can make the choice to treat yourself with understanding and care.

As Dr. Kristin Neff, an associate professor at the University of Texas at Austin, says, "When we feel inadequate, our self-concept is threatened, so we attack the problem—ourselves!"[5] Remember the amygdala hijacking from chapter 1? When we instinctually react to the perceived danger associated with something going wrong, self-criticism is often the first reaction. Instead of triggering this stress response when we feel threatened, a mindfulness practice teaches us to intentionally activate our body's calming response and treat ourselves kindly instead.

A pioneer in the field of self-compassion, Dr. Neff has created a three-step self-compassion practice to enable us to soothe ourselves when distressed.

1. *Be mindful.* Notice when you're struggling, and acknowledge that you're in emotional pain. Talk to yourself as you would to a good friend: tell yourself things like "This is hard" or "I'm struggling right now."
2. *Acknowledge our common humanity.* When you notice yourself suffering, instead of separating yourself from others, remind yourself that suffering is part of the human experience and that you share these feelings with every other person on the planet. Say phrases

to yourself like "Suffering is part of life" or "Everyone feels this way sometimes."

3. ***Give yourself kindness and soothing physical touch.*** You might put your hand on your heart or gently clasp your hands together and say, "May I accept myself as I am" or "May I have the patience to get through this time" or "It's going to be okay." Allow your warm touch to reinforce your warm words.[6]

Although we humans are wired to pay attention to the negative (the negativity bias mentioned in chapter 1), it's reassuring to know that self-compassion can be learned, and that when practiced regularly, it has lasting positive effects. Studies show that people who took a self-compassion class designed by Professor Neff increased their levels of self-compassion by 43 percent. They experienced more compassion toward others, more social connection, more life satisfaction, and more happiness, while also experiencing less depression, anxiety, and stress.[7]

PONDER THIS

In the spirit of developing resiliency and well-being, list three things you can do for yourself this coming week.

1. _____

2. _____

3. _____

The Loving-Kindness Meditation is one of the most popular forms of meditation in the Buddhist tradition. It's a method for developing compassion and cultivating feelings of tenderness, kindness, and friendliness for ourselves and others. With practice, it increases our capacity for forgiveness and connection to others. This is a variation on the traditional Loving-Kindness meditation and focuses specifically on generating good feelings toward your teen and yourself.

LOVING-KINDNESS MEDITATION

Sit comfortably, with your back straight and both feet planted firmly on the ground. Close your eyes and rest your hands in your lap. Notice the weight of your body in your seat and the feeling of the air on your skin. Let any tightness or tension in your body drain away. Allow your body to rest and relax.

Bring your focus mindfully to your breath. Take several slow, deep breaths, inhaling through the nose and exhaling through the mouth. As you breathe deeply, notice where you feel the movement of your breath most. What sensations are present in your body as you breathe in and out, easily and effortlessly?

Bring your attention to your chest and heart. Open and soften your heart, as you allow yourself to connect with your natural inner feelings of kindness and compassion for others. Invite these loving feelings to radiate throughout your body.

Shift your attention to your teen. Imagine your teen is standing in front of you, and you are speaking gently and quietly to them as you would to a frightened or injured child. Silently say, "May you be safe and protected." Take another breath. On the next breath, say, "May you be happy." Take another breath, and with this breath say, "May you be healthy and well." Take another breath, and with this one, say, "May you live with ease." Pick one of these phrases, or make up your own, and put all your heart into it each time you say it silently to your teen. Let kindness, compassion, and warm wishes flow through you. Repeat this phrase, as if singing a lullaby to a baby.

Now shift your attention to yourself. You can focus on your whole self or some part that needs care and attention, such as the site of a physical injury or a feeling of emotional pain.

Imagine speaking gently and quietly to yourself, as a mother speaks to her frightened or injured child. Use the phrase "May I be safe and protected." Take another breath, and now say, "May I be happy." Take a slow, deep breath. On this breath, say, "May I be healthy and well." Take another breath. With the next breath, say, "May I live with ease." Pick one of these phrases that works for you, or make up your own. Then put all your heart into it each time you speak it to yourself. Let kindness, compassion, and warm wishes flow through you. Repeat this phrase, as if singing a lullaby to a baby.

As this meditation comes to a close, notice the state of your heart and your mind. Now keep your eyes closed and return your attention to your breathing. And when you're ready, open your eyes and return your focus to the room.

If you would rather listen to a guided meditation, please visit https://mindfulparentingofteens.com/mindful-meditations/.

What was that Loving-Kindness Meditation like for you?

_____

_____

_____

_____

_____

_____

_____

_____

_____

_____

_____

_____

_____

_____

_____

_____

_____

_____

Know that you can use these loving-kindness phrases whenever you wish and directed to whomever you wish. You can use them with yourself, your children, your spouse, your friends, your coworkers, all beings, even people in your life whom you find difficult. When doing the Loving-Kindness Meditation, you might experience many different emotions—even sadness, anger, or irritation. If you do, simply observe these feelings without judgment. It's common for all sorts of thoughts and emotions to come up when you practice loving-kindness.

CLOSING

What emotions most often impact your interactions with your teen? (Use the list of from earlier in the chapter as a guide.) What are the physical sensations associated with those emotions?

_____

_____

_____

_____

_____

_____

_____

_____

_____

_____

_____

_____

_____

_____

_____

_____

_____

_____

The Guest House
This being human is a guest house.
Every morning a new arrival.

A joy, a depression, a meanness,
some momentary awareness comes
as an unexpected visitor.

Welcome and entertain them all!
Even if they are a crowd of sorrows,
who violently sweep your house
empty of its furniture,
still, treat each guest honorably.
He may be clearing you out
for some new delight.

The dark thought, the shame, the malice,
meet them at the door laughing, and invite them in.

Be grateful for whoever comes,
because each has been sent
as a guide from beyond.

—Jalaluddin Rumi, "The Guest House,"
translated by Coleman Barks in The Essential
Rumi, New Expanded Edition

CHAPTER 5

The Power of Mindful Conversation: Strategies for Skillful Communication with Your Teen

Speak only endearing speech,
speech that is welcomed.
Speech when it brings no evil
to others
is pleasant.

—Ven. Vaṅgīsa (disciple of the Buddha), from the
Subhasita Sutta, translated by Thānissaro Bhikkhu

PONDER THIS

What would it be like if you argued less with your teen?

_____

_____

_____

_____

_____

_____

_____

_____

_____

_____

_____

_____

_____

_____

The tween and teen years inevitably bring more confrontation and disagreements. When we ask the above question in our workshop, parents tell us that if there were less conflict, their homes would be quieter, calmer, sweeter, and even more fun. We can't eliminate the conflict with our teens (because of their developmental mission to drive us away), but there are ways we can communicate with them that can reduce some of the conflict.

REDUCING REACTIVITY TO INCREASE POSITIVITY

When talking with your teen, how often do you get frustrated because you just can't get through to them? Does it seem like your every request falls on deaf ears? Do you feel like no matter how important what you have to say is, all your teen hears is the *wah-wah-wah* Charlie Brown voice coming out of your mouth?

Welcome to communicating with a teen! In this chapter, we'll focus on being more mindful about the language and tone you use, because this can influence how your conversations go. This chapter will provide concrete strategies for staying calmer and less reactive. Being more conscious about how you communicate with your teen can lead to less contention and more positivity in your home.

COMMON FLASH POINTS

Differences of opinion are a natural part of any relationship, but with teens, it can feel like *every* interaction becomes a fight. At its foundation, an argument is a power struggle between your desires and those of your teenager. You have different opinions about what should happen, and it's unlikely that arguing your position will bring your teen around—or vice versa.

There are two common conversations, or flash points, that cause tension between parents and teens: (1) saying no and (2) making a request. Tell a teen they can't go out with their friend, or ask them to put down their phone when they talk to you, and . . . bam! Let the argument begin. These interactions can escalate surprisingly quickly. Before you know it, you're locked in a screaming match you never intended to be in. So instead of trying to convince your teen that you're right, try some of these communication tools to help you get through flash-point conversations more calmly and adroitly.

SAYING NO: A FOUR-STEP PROCESS

Here's a simple—but not necessarily easy—four-step process for *saying no.*

> **Step 1: Validate.** The first step is to validate your teenager's desires and feelings. Let them know that you hear what they want and understand the feelings behind their wish. This establishes empathy and creates a connection with your teen, even if you ultimately deny the request.

> **Step 2: State a clear preference to deny the request.** You've started the conversation by validating your teen's point of view. The second step is to clearly state your preference not to do what they're asking. If you can express your preference in a calm, neutral

voice, all the better. This lets the teen know up front what your position is.

Step 3: Listen to the argument and decide whether you're willing to compromise. Sometimes you may be willing to compromise because circumstances evolve or your teen makes a compelling argument—or in order to avert conflict with your teen and pick your battles mindfully. For instance, you might not *like* it if your daughter dyes her hair some awful, unnatural color, but you're willing to let her experiment in this way, while you draw the line at body piercing. Each parent has to decide which compromises they are and aren't willing to make, based on their own beliefs and standards. You may decide to compromise more as your adolescent gets older. For instance, you may not be ready for your ninth grader to go to a concert with his friends, but by the time he's in eleventh grade, you might allow this privilege. If you are willing to compromise, tell your teen succinctly why, and let them know what the new expectation is.

Step 4: If you're not willing to compromise, stand firm with your "no." It's critically important that once you've decided, you do not back down from your "no" position. If you relent after a barrage of arguments, your teen learns that if they just keep arguing long enough, they can wear you down and eventually you'll cave in.

What would this look like? Say you've agreed to let your daughter hang out with a group of kids at a friend's house on a Friday night, with the provision that you will pick her up at eleven o'clock. Just before eleven, you get a call from her, begging you to come at midnight instead. Let's put the four-step process to work in this situation.

> ***Step 1: Validate.*** Let her know you heard her by saying something like "It sounds like you're having fun. I know you really want to stay because you're having a good time with your friends and it feels like you just got there."

> ***Step 2: State a clear preference to deny the request.*** Clearly state your preference not to come pick her up later. You might say, "I can see why you'd want to stay at your friend's until midnight and have me pick you up later, but I'm not willing to do that."

> ***Step 3: Listen to the argument and decide if you're willing to compromise.*** If you're willing to compromise and pick her up an hour later, you could say, "Okay, I'm willing to compromise and come an hour later because you've shown you can be responsible in these situations."

> ***Step 4: If you're not willing to compromise, stand firm with your "no."*** You might say, "No, that later time doesn't work for me. I'll come get you at eleven as we agreed." Remember, if you've decided to say no, relenting after an argument trains your teen that if they're persistent enough, they can wear you down.

Be aware that even with this script, your teen will put up resistance. It's their job, after all, to oppose you. So expect this resistance and bring out your disengagement strategies (reiterated at the end of this section).

MAKING A REQUEST: A THREE-STEP PROCESS

The other dynamic that is sure to provoke conflict with your teen is making a request of them. Again, here's a simple—but not necessarily easy—three-step process for making a request.

> ***Step 1: Brief justification (optional).*** Although it's not always necessary, it may be helpful to provide an explanation for your request. If you explain, do it briefly and succinctly. By bottom-lining your request and not spinning out into the multiple reasons you want them to comply, you keep the interaction focused on *your* agenda, which is to get the task completed.

> ***Step 2: Make a direct, specific request.*** Next, make a specific request so the desired outcome isn't open to interpretation. Make your request as clear as possible. Language like "I'm asking you to . . ." or "I'd appreciate it if you . . ." can soften the blow.

> ***Step 3: Appreciation statement.*** We often forget to thank our children for doing something, because . . . well, they should have done it without our having to ask in the first place! Rather than showing appreciation, we resent having to nag them to get it done—so the idea of expressing gratitude doesn't always come naturally. But acknowledging their efforts (even

when we're hard-pressed to feel grateful) can create a small connection in the moment and build equity in the long-term relationship.

Here's an example of how to make a request:

> *Step 1: Brief justification (optional).* Start by succinctly summarizing the situation. For instance: "We have friends coming over for dinner tonight, so the house needs to be presentable for our guests."

> *Step 2: Make a direct, specific request.* Make your request clear and specific, using softening language if possible. In this example, it might sound something like "Since we have guests coming over for dinner tonight, and the house needs to be clean, I'm asking you to please clean your room within the next hour."

> *Step 3: Appreciation statement.* Remember to acknowledge their efforts with a statement like "Thank you, I really appreciate your help" or "I know you didn't want to do this, so I'm grateful you cleaned your room."

EXPECT RESISTANCE

You've made your skillful denial or request. Now be prepared for your teen's resistance—which will be as vigorous as it is inevitable. Teens generally feel indignant about the demands placed on them (looking at you, "baby self"). They will resist and procrastinate. "I'll do it later" usually means "It's not going to happen."[1] This opposition is what causes much of the conflict between parents and teens, so we return to the disengagement strategies of chapter 4 to deal with the defiance after you've gone through your script.

STRATEGIC DISENGAGEMENT REVISITED

As we discussed previously, disengaging can be an effective communication strategy when things are starting to heat up. Saying no or making a request is sure to get your teenager's amygdala firing and incite resistance. To avoid having *your* amygdala fired up as well, try disengaging. Again, you are not disengaging from your child, but instead disengaging from the *conflict*. As the conflict becomes a power struggle, you're better off saying your piece and disengaging. Let's review those disengagement strategies here:

1. Pause and Breathe
2. Talk Less—"Broken Record"
3. Stop Talking—"Last Word"
4. Walk Away

Teens are very clever at confronting you and making you the bad guy. They are so good at this, in fact, that the initial point of the conversation can easily get lost in their allegations of unfairness and bad parenting. These disengagement strategies will help you stay on point, rather than getting sidetracked by your teen's arguments, attacks, and name-calling.

Here are a few other good communication strategies to help you keep cool in the face of your teen's resistance.

STICK TO THE MISSION

In *The Blessing of a B Minus*, Dr. Wendy Mogel advises parents to "stay focused on the mission" and not get derailed by the avalanche of arguments a teen will marshal to prove they're right.[2] Dr. Mogel offers words and phrases that help us ignore distractions and rudeness and stay on point, including:

- Nevertheless . . .
- Regardless . . .
- I remember saying no about this.
- That's not the issue.
- I'm not going to change my mind about this.
- My decision is final.
- I've thought about it and the answer is no.
- I'm not ready for that [concert, party, outfit, etc.].

MUTUAL VALIDATION

Use the language of *mutual validation* to soften an unpopular decision or request. With mutual validation, you acknowledge where the other person is coming from while stating your own preference. It might sound like this: "I understand that you want to play violent video games. On my end, my job as a parent is to protect you from certain images until you're older and can understand it better. I'd prefer to play a board game with you." Or: "I understand that you don't think you need a curfew and that you're helping friends get home safely, but setting a curfew helps me sleep better and keeps you safer." This language doesn't make either person right or wrong, yet it acknowledges each person's point of view. In other words, this technique validates your teen's perspective without actually agreeing with it. It simply says, "I understand you feel that way. And I feel this way."

PARTIAL APOLOGY

Another softening technique, suggested by Anthony Wolf, is a partial apology. With a partial apology, you concede that your teen is offended by something you did or said, but you continue to stand firm in your expectation or request. Again, you're acknowledging their stance without invalidating yours.[3] For example: "I'm sorry it sounded like I was accusing you of being lazy. That's not what I meant. You need to stay home this weekend to study for your finals next week."

PUTTING IT ALL TOGETHER

Here's a simple scenario to show how you could use some of the communication tools we've been discussing.

From your perspective as the parent, you don't ask a lot of your children, but you do have certain rules and standards in your family about helping around the house. Your teen has been working on a report for school and has left papers all over the dining-room table. You need her to clear them away so the family can eat dinner at the table. You'll make your request, then expect and prepare for resistance.

If you're the teenager, you've had a really long day already, with a full day of school, sports, and your extremely active social life. You just need some time at home to chill out without being nagged by your parent. You don't want to clear the stuff off the table right now, and you're annoyed that your parent doesn't get this. Why are they always so uptight? Is it so hard for them to understand that you'll get to it later?

> YOU: *Honey, we're going to eat dinner in the dining room tonight* [BRIEF JUSTIFICATION]. *I'd really appreciate it if you could clear your papers off the table so we can eat there at six* [DIRECT, SPECIFIC REQUEST]. *Thank you for your help* [APPRECIATION STATEMENT].

> TEEN: *Mom, really?* [EYE ROLL] *I just got home from school. I'll do it later.*

> YOU: *I know you just got home and don't want to clear the table, but I really need you to do this before dinner so we're sure it happens* [MUTUAL VALIDATION].

> TEEN: *I have too much homework to do. I can't do it right now.*

> YOU: *I'm sorry you've got so much schoolwork—that's a drag. Nevertheless, I still need you clear the papers before dinner* [STICK TO THE MISSION, PARTIAL APOLOGY, BROKEN RECORD].

> TEEN: *Why do I have to do all the work around here? You're the one who cares about this. You've got a weird obsession about eating at the dining-room table.*

Why don't you clear the papers off of the table?!

YOU: *That's not the issue. Your papers need to be cleared* [STICK TO THE MISSION, BROKEN RECORD].

TEEN: *I hate you. I don't want to deal with this!*

YOU: *Regardless, the table needs to be cleared off* [STICK TO THE MISSION, BROKEN RECORD].

TEEN: *This is so unfair!*

YOU: *Papers, please* [TALK LESS].

TEEN: *Fine! I'll do it, but you're the meanest mom ever.*

YOU: *Thanks, sweetheart. I appreciate your help* [APPRECIATION STATEMENT].

HOW TO RECOVER AFTER YOU HAVE A CONFLICT

Despite our best intentions, we all blow it sometimes! We lose it, we say things we wish we hadn't, we feel horrible. Rather than going down the rabbit hole of guilt, recrimination, and despair, I recommend you use the tool of *recovery*.

Recovery is the ability to bounce back from a conflict, so you can get your relationship with your teen—and yourself— on track again. It requires mindfulness to observe your own emotions, see that they're heading downhill, and have the distance and objectivity to not be overwhelmed by them. It requires noticing that you're in a bad place and doing what you can to get yourself back to equilibrium. This is not pretending that the conflict didn't happen or that the emotions don't exist. Instead, you're making a conscious decision to put the incident behind you and not let the negative thoughts and feelings take over. The aim is to move through the conflict so you can regain your center and be the parent you want to be in the next moment.

Sports psychology offers us a helpful analogy for the importance of recovering from an argument. After all, we all know that sparring with a teen can require the presence of mind and endurance of an elite athlete! Performance psychologist Jim Loehr and his colleagues studied what distinguishes award-winning tennis players from others. After reviewing hours of match play, they found that the difference between champions and other players was the best players' ability to recover between points. The top players had rituals—such as how they held their bodies when they walked back to the baseline, how they breathed, and how they talked to themselves between points—that lowered their heart rates and refocused their attention so they were relaxed and ready for the next ball coming over the net.[4]

Identify your own recovery tools that you can use after a conflict with your teen. The first step is to notice your turbulent thoughts and feelings and choose to recover rather than getting stuck replaying what happened and going into a downward spiral. The second step is to develop your own rituals to help you get back to center so you're ready for the next "ball" coming over the net.

Some recovery tactics include:

- Taking three deep belly breaths
- Meditating
- Going for a walk
- Making a cup of tea
- Calling a friend
- Counting backward from ten to one
- Getting outdoors
- Distracting yourself with work
- Doing yoga
- Taking the dog out
- Listening to music
- Playing the piano
- Commiserating with your partner
- Apologizing to your teen

Remember, this is not pretending that the argument didn't happen. If the conflict is over something important, it can be useful, even necessary, to wait until you're feeling calmer to revisit the situation and think through what you need to communicate to your teen and how you might have handled it better. You can always try a "do-over" after you've had a chance to clear your head and ground yourself.

Think of recovery as part of the arc of the conflict. There's a disagreement, arguing ensues, things escalate, you strategically disengage, the argument dies down, and later, you recover from the blowup. Having your own recovery strategies at hand when this occurs can help the recovery process go more quickly. It also models for your children how they can learn to recover from conflict themselves. And it shows them that conflict itself is not catastrophic. Family members can disagree, argue, and then ultimately reconnect.

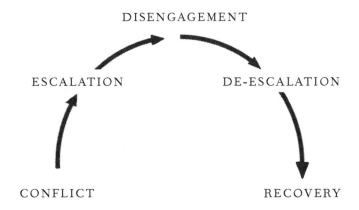

DISENGAGEMENT

ESCALATION

DE-ESCALATION

CONFLICT

RECOVERY

PONDER THIS

List some recovery strategies you could use after an argument with your teen.

_____

_____

_____

_____

_____

_____

_____

_____

_____

_____

_____

_____

_____

INCREASE POSITIVITY
BY EXPRESSING AFFECTION,
GRATITUDE, AND KINDNESS

When our children were younger, it was easy to love them wholeheartedly. Now that they're oppositional teens, it can be harder to feel that unqualified affection. But the truth is that they need our unconditional love as much as ever. Although teenagers may not *act* like it, they do want to know that we love them even when they're rejecting us *(hello, separation and individuation!)*. With mindfulness, we can intentionally show them we care even if we feel like we're under attack.

One way is to remember to point out when they're doing something right. Professor Barbara Fredrickson, of the University of North Carolina at Chapel Hill, has spent over twenty years studying positivity and found that in order to flourish, human beings should experience (over time) a ratio of 3-to-1 positive to negative experiences in daily life. When we are experiencing this positivity ratio, research shows that not only do we feel better, we're more creative, resilient, and open to possibilities.[5] Stop for a minute and think about what your ratio might be like living with a teen. Face it, a lot of teen behavior leaves us feeling low. One way to increase positivity in a genuine way is to make an effort to catch them doing things *right* and to appreciate them for their good qualities and behaviors. Acknowledgments like "Great job getting your math homework finished before dinner" or "You're really a kind and loyal friend" go a long way toward increasing our positivity ratio, lifting our mood, and building goodwill in the relationship.

Another idea, borrowed from Wendy Mogel, to increase positivity is to say yes to your teen's requests *with enthusiasm—* especially those you know you're going to have to do anyway.

"Sure, I'd be happy to drive you across town to your violin lesson!" or "Yes, absolutely, go have fun with your friends at the basketball game!" or "Going out? Can I give you some money for dinner?"[6]

Anthony Wolf also provides some great advice about staying upbeat in the face of snarkiness.[7] You don't want to let your teen's sullen mood set the tone for every interaction. For example, imagine your teen walks into the kitchen in the morning, takes one look at the beautiful breakfast you cooked, and says, "Ugh, bacon and eggs again. I hate bacon and eggs." Your response might be "Good morning, sunshine! Don't you love bacon and eggs? It's my favorite breakfast. If it were up to me, I'd eat bacon and eggs for every meal!" Or maybe you pop your head into her bedroom while she's doing homework and say, "I love you, honey." When she responds with "Dad, go away," you say, "I still love you!" To which she might respond (trying not to smile), "Dad, you're so weird." Success! The point is that the teen years don't always feel fun, so sometimes acting silly keeps *your* mood upbeat and the interactions lighter.

Another thing that happens as our kids enter their teen years is that we don't have as much physical contact with them as we did when they were younger. Many teens don't want a lot of touching from us. In fact, they may tell you they don't want you to touch them at all, and it's important to pay attention to that. But a quick hug or a gentle hand on their back is an easy way to connect with them and show them that you care. Again, it's best if you don't have any expectation that your teen will act like they like it. In fact, they may tell you they *don't* like it: "Mom, stop it. You don't have to hug me all the time!" Regardless, keep looking for opportunities to make those quick physical gestures that communicate affection. And every now and then, you might go in for a big hug and actually find yourself getting one back!

Also, remember to say "thank you" for the things they do without your having to ask them. This can be anything from "Thank you for coming on that family outing—we enjoyed having you with us" to "Thank you for feeding the cat" (even though it's their *job* and they do it every day). Say thank you with no expectation of a response, so you aren't disappointed if there isn't one. You do this so you *feel* more appreciative, which supports a connection with your teen.

Recent research has shown that performing one intentional act of kindness a day for seven days increases one's level of happiness.[8] This is true whether the recipient of the kind act is someone you know and care about or a stranger. What if you chose to perform one daily act of kindness for your tween or teen? Could you bring him a cup of tea at his desk while he's studying? Offer a shoulder massage at the end of the day? Make his favorite dessert . . . just because? Try this experiment for one week and notice if there's an impact on your teen—or on you. Notice whether your level of happiness increases.

Finally, never underestimate the impact of simply reassuring your teen that things are going to be all right. When your teen is getting anxious or upset, it can be helpful just to say the words "It's okay." Saying these words out loud can calm them down, and, equally important, it can help calm *you* down. It reminds you to put things in perspective, be patient, and know that everything is probably going to work itself out in the end. This eases anxiety and puts you in a more helpful, creative frame of mind.

MINDFUL LISTENING: A PARENT'S SUPERPOWER

As simple as it sounds, we spend a lot of time *talking* to our teens and not nearly as much time *listening* to them. And this isn't just the case with our kids. We often have whole conversations where we're partially listening to the other person, but also partially paying attention to the chatter in our own heads. Our minds get distracted from the conversation by our judgments, our comparisons, and our thinking ahead to the next brilliant thing we're going to say.

Mindful listening is a different way of having a conversation, where we intentionally focus on the other person and listen with open curiosity. We slow down our mental chatter and pay attention to the other person so we can really hear what they're saying—not just the words, but the underlying mood and emotions. When listening mindfully, we're not providing analysis or advice, but hearing the other person's words and making an effort to understand their perspective. This kind of listening doesn't require us to solve, lecture, or share our vast knowledge on all manner of subjects. It just asks us to be fully present, giving our complete attention to the other person, moment to moment, without judgment—and when our mind wanders, gently bringing it back to the conversation.

. Of course, mindful listening is not the only way to communicate with a teen. As parents, we often need to provide information or offer an assessment of a situation. But when we make a conscious effort to really listen to what our teen is saying, it can change the quality of the conversation and deepen our connection.

So how do you have a mindful conversation? It starts with an intention to be interested, respectful, and empathetic. You set the intention to suspend judgment and focus your attention on what your teen is saying. Rather than entering the conversation with your opinions ready and arguments fired up, you choose to approach your teen with an open heart and an open mind. You become aware of your judgments and stories and observe them with detachment, rather than being driven to respond from these thoughts. You ask open-ended questions that give them the chance to tell their version of the story.

The best open-ended questions begin with "How," "What," and "Who." Avoid those that start with "Why," which can shut people down. For example, imagine how differently these two questions might be received: "What can you do to improve your soccer game?" As opposed to "Why can't you get better at soccer?"

Second, it's important to have an open, kind mindset. Most of us have strongly held ideas about how our children should be and act. There's nothing wrong with establishing clear rules and upholding standards. In fact, a big part of our job is to guide our children based on our priorities and values. But coming into a conversation with fixed assumptions about how things should be can close down the conversation before it's even started. Sometimes we just need to be curious about what our teen is saying. When they realize we're not judging and evaluating them, they're more likely to tell us what's really going on.

Mindful listening also asks us to be generous and assume that our teen has good intentions. Often, arguments become explosive because we think the worst about our kids. This is human nature and doesn't happen just with our children. While we're inclined to ascribe good intentions to ourselves, we don't always assume those same good intentions in others. For instance, we might excuse ourselves for being late to an event because we know we tried hard to get there but time just got away from us. And yet, in the absence of full information, we make up intent and tend to judge another person negatively. We're more likely to assume that someone else is late meeting us at that same event because they're irresponsible and don't value our time. Mindful listening turns this around and asks us to assume that our teen, just like us, is doing the best they can, and to start the conversation from a kindhearted, non-judgmental point of view.

It's also helpful not to put your teen on the spot. Teens don't like to have one-on-one, eyeball-to-eyeball conversations with their parents. You may have better luck getting them to open up to you if you don't come at them head-on. Sometimes it's easier to talk if you're doing something else, like walking the dog or riding in a car together. It's easier for teens (and many adults too) to share more openly when they don't feel like they're under the microscope.

Finally, it can be very effective to respond to what your teen is saying in a composed, neutral way. This is a variation on the "Talk Less" strategy from chapter 4. When you're practicing mindful listening, sometimes the most powerful thing you can do is to hold your initial reaction in check. If you ask a teen an open-ended question and they respond in a way that surprises or upsets you, you can pause, breathe, and say as little as possible. Saying something like "Hmmm, that's interesting" or "Tell me what you mean" or just mirroring back the words they used can keep the conversation going and prevent it from escalating. Here's an example of a conversation that might happen after school one day:

YOU: *How did things go today?*

TEEN: *Fine.*

YOU: *Anything interesting going on at school?*

TEEN: *No.*

[AWKWARD SILENCE]

YOU: *Are you still planning to get together with Maddy this afternoon?*

TEEN: *Nope.*

[MORE AWKWARD SILENCE]

TEEN: *Actually, Maddy can't hang out with me.*

YOU [IN YOUR HEAD]: *Oh no, not another problem with Maddy. That girl is a nightmare. She's always excluding my daughter. I can't stand that kid.*

YOU [OUT LOUD]: *Oh . . . What's up?*

TEEN: *Maddy is grounded. Last Saturday, she told her parents she was going to Kira's house but went to Jack's instead. She had some beer and got busted by her parents. Now she can't hang out with any of her friends for a month.*

YOU [IN YOUR HEAD]: *WTF? Are you kidding me?! They're starting to drink*

*already! OMG, I knew this was com-
ing but didn't think it would happen so
soon. Is my daughter drinking? I need
to lock up all the alcohol in the house!*

You *[out loud]*: Wow. [PAUSE] *What
happened?*

TEEN: *Jack's parents were away, so he had
a party. She went and had too much to
drink. Her parents had to go pick her
up, because she got sick. Everyone at
school is talking about it. I'm kind of
worried about her.*

YOU [IN YOUR HEAD]: *I really need to
have the talk again about drinking,
and how unhealthy it is for a developing brain. And we need to revisit what
to do if she gets in this situation. I need
to remind her that if she needs me to,
I'll come pick her up no matter the time
or situation. OMG, should I talk to her
now? Should I wait until I can do it
with her dad? I'm not being a responsible parent if I don't tell her what I think
about underage drinking and lying to
parents and . . .*

YOU [OUT LOUD]: *Hmm, you're worried
about her . . .*

You get the idea. In the moment, you notice that you have many thoughts, emotions, and reactions, but you choose to not make your opinions known. Because if you don't jump in with all *your* ideas about what happened, you might have an interesting talk about your *teen's* thoughts about the situation. Sometimes your teen just needs to vent. If this is the case, you can ask her, "Do you want me to respond to what you're saying, or just listen?" Managing your reactivity also shows your teen that she can have a difficult conversation with you—without your freaking out. This is just one example of how active listening and talking less may open things up for your teen to say more.

Although this chapter is about being skillful in our external dialogues with our teens, it's important to be mindful of our internal dialogues as well. As we saw in chapter 3, our behavior and attitudes are often driven by our thoughts and judgments. In the next meditation, we're intentionally cultivating messages that affirm us as parents and provide compassion for ourselves through the difficult times.

PARENTING MANTRAS MEDITATION

Start this Mantras Meditation by relaxing in your chair and observing the effortlessness of your breathing as you gently inhale and exhale.

In this meditation we'll be repeating several man-tras about parenting. A mantra is a word or phrase that you can repeat out loud or in silence. Repeating a mantra helps focus your attention and anchor the mind in concentration. It's a positive affirmation to nourish your spirit and help you let go of negative or agitated thinking. We say these mantras during the relaxed state of meditation so that they will sink deeply into our being.

If you can, relax into these phrases as you're saying them, and see if you can really feel what the mantra expresses as you speak it. Perhaps you can coordinate saying the mantras with the inhale and exhale of your breath.

Start with the mantra "I can only control myself." Breathe gently and slowly and repeat the mantra to yourself. It's important to remember that our teens have their own will and, as much as we can support and guide them, we can't actually control them. Since the only person you can control is yourself, it's more effective to focus on your own behavior so you can stay more calm and loving. Repeat the mantra: "I can only control myself."

Now say the mantra "I will pause before I react." Repeat it to yourself. Teens know just how to push our buttons. Rather than reacting without thinking, give yourself a moment to pause before you react so you can choose your words or actions with care. Repeat the phrase: "I will pause before I react."

Now say the mantra "The house will soon be quiet." Sometimes it's hard to deal with the day-to-day, rough-and-tumble of parenting. But it can be useful to remember that your child won't always be living in your home, slamming the doors, yelling at their siblings, or arguing with you about every little thing. Knowing that this argument will pass—and, as important, this phase will pass too—can provide some healthy perspective. Repeat the phrase "The house will soon be quiet" and let it sink into your core. If your mind wanders as you're doing this meditation, gently bring it back to the mantras and focus on saying them again.

Now say the mantra "My teen is loved and supported." None of us want our children to struggle, but disappointment and hardships are inevitable. Their friends will be mean; they'll fail a test; they won't make the team or get the part in the play. But we can reassure ourselves by knowing that our intentions are good, and that what we want most for our teens is their well-being. They're getting love and support from us despite whatever else is happening in their lives. Say the phrase: "My teen is loved and supported."

Now say the mantra "I'm doing the best I can." When things don't go well, we can let self-judgment and doubt creep in. We look around and see only other families that appear to have it all figured out. Instead of comparing ourselves to others or questioning our abilities as parents, using this mantra reminds us that we're bringing our best intentions to the job of parenting. Let this mantra sink in deeply: "I'm doing the best I can."

We'll end the meditation with this final mantra: "I am not alone." Breathe deeply and keep in mind that the struggles you're having as a parent are not yours alone. All of us have our moments of doubt and difficulty. When we're feeling challenged, we often isolate ourselves rather than connecting with others when we need it most. Remembering that there are others facing the same challenges helps us maintain our equanimity during these vexing teen years. Repeat the phrase, feeling it deeply. "I am not alone."

You can say these mantras whenever you want— during a formal meditation or informally while going about your day.

We'll close this meditation by breathing steadily and slowly while repeating each mantra:

"I can only control myself."

"I will pause before I react."

"The house will soon be quiet."

"My teen is loved and supported."

"I'm doing the best I can."

"I am not alone."

Now turn your attention back to your breathing. And when you're ready, open your eyes and bring your attention back to the room.

If you would rather listen to a guided meditation, please visit https://mindfulparentingofteens.com/mindful-meditations/.

What was that Parenting Mantras Meditation like for you?

_____

_____

_____

_____

_____

_____

_____
_____
_____
_____
_____
_____
_____
_____
_____
_____
_____
_____
_____
_____
_____
_____
_____
_____

The Parenting Mantras Meditation can help us remember what we're in control of and what we're not. Reminding ourselves of these truths allows us to look at our current worries from a different point of view and gives us multiple ways to think about what's happening with our teen. Depending on what's going on with them at any given time, different mantras will resonate more than others. The practice is to remember to use the mantras when you're feeling anxious, overwhelmed, and in need of grounding.

CLOSING

What one or two strategies will you use this week to be less reactive and more positive in your communication with your teen?

_____

_____

_____

_____

_____

_____

_____

_____

_____

_____

_____

_____

CHAPTER 6

The Power of Accepting What You Can't Change About Your Teen

We must be willing to get rid of the life we've planned,
so as to have the life that is waiting for us.

—Joseph Campbell, quoted in Reflections on the
Art of Living: A Joseph Campbell Companion

PONDER THIS

When you imagine the characteristics of the ideal parent, what
qualities would you want this ideal parent to have?

_____

_____

_____

_____

_____

_____

_____

_____

_____

When we ask this question in our workshop, participants respond with words like *supportive, loving, caring, good listener, present, spontaneous, wise, helpful, optimistic, nurturing, compassionate, strong, fun,* and *funny*. And yet, often the qualities we bring to the job are more along the lines of judging, demanding, helicoptering, and so on. These qualities are usually formed from good intentions—from wanting good things for our children and encouraging them to do and be their best.

PONDER THIS

How many of these desirable parenting qualities are you demonstrating with your own children? What would you like to do more of?

_____

_____

_____

_____

_____

_____

_____

_____

_____

_____

_____

What qualities would you like to display less of?

_____

_____

_____

_____

_____

_____

_____

_____

_____

_____

It can be helpful to step back and ask yourself if the expectations you're holding are realistic—or even in your child's best interest. This takes courage: to see the child you have, to love and support that person, and to let go of the assumptions you hold that may not serve them.

ACCEPTING THE CHILD YOU HAVE

Mindfulness meditation helps you become a loving, impartial observer of your own experience; it allows you to be fully present in the moment, and to accept what's here with curiosity and acceptance rather than judgment or criticism. It requires training yourself to see what's going on inside of you—whether it's sensations in the body or thoughts or emotions—without trying to change them. This takes practice and skill. But when you do it, when you accept what's there and investigate it with openness, you can realize you are not defined by your thoughts and emotions, and that leads to greater freedom and ease. When you take each moment as it comes and are able to be with it fully, without resistance, you can find that the sensations, thoughts, and emotions subside more quickly. Acceptance doesn't mean that you have to like the situation or passively let it be. You can still take action to change things, but you're doing so from a place of acceptance rather than resistance or overidentification. So what does this look like in real life?

Imagine you are on your way home from work, and you get stuck in unusually snarled traffic. You can rage against the other cars, rant at your fellow drivers, or blame yourself for not leaving the office earlier to avoid the mess. Or instead of focusing on how it shouldn't be this way or how much you can't stand it, you could acknowledge that bad traffic is your current reality and go from there. Maybe you call home and explain that you'll be late. Perhaps you choose to drive home by a different route. Or maybe you put on a podcast and decide to enjoy the unexpected extra time in the car. Refusing to accept reality doesn't change the situation, it just adds to the pain—while accepting what is, without judgment, allows us to move into a wiser, more creative frame of mind.

In parenting terms, it's normal to have expectations about how we want our kids to be. We may not think much about it, but most of us have firmly held views about the qualities and behaviors we want our children to exhibit. And although they may have many of these qualities, they probably also have some we wish they didn't possess. Whether we like it or not, our kids are born with a unique blend of temperament, strengths, and weaknesses that we can (maybe) influence, but can't necessarily change. Parents of teens sometimes tend to hyperfocus on the qualities they don't like. We might wish for the teen to be a certain way—academically stronger, a better athlete or musician, more popular, or more engaged with the larger world, for example. We project our own wishes and desires onto our kids and can get caught up in "shoulds," "coulds," and "oughts" that may not reflect who our child really is. These often-unconscious expectations cause us disappointment and suffering, because our image of who we want our children to be may not match up with reality. By resisting the reality of who our child is, we, and our child, experience real pain and suffering. And while we still might feel sadness or disappointment, if we choose instead to accept them as they truly are, it allows us to soften our resistance and bring more compassion and connection to the relationship.

RADICAL ACCEPTANCE

Radical acceptance rests on letting go of the illusion of control and a willingness to notice and accept things just as they are right now, without judging.

—Katy Butler, "On the Borderline,"
describing the work of Marsha Linehan, founder
of dialectical behavior therapy (DBT)

One way to move from judgment, disappointment, and resistance to acceptance is to practice *radical acceptance*. Taken from Zen philosophy, radical acceptance requires us to accept what is rather than worrying about how it could be. It's saying yes to life just as it is. It's "radical" because it's complete and total; the aim is to accept completely—with your mind, heart, and body.

Remember when we talked in chapter 2 about the Buddha's Four Noble Truths? One of these truths is that suffering is caused by our resistance to our circumstances. Refusing to accept a situation doesn't change it, but can intensify our emotional distress. When we choose to accept reality as it is, rather than fight it because it isn't what we'd hoped, this gives us freedom to see what's there and make choices from a more realistic point of view. When things aren't the way we want, we may feel threatened and angry, often blaming others. This prevents us from seeing what's really happening and the opportunities that exist. Instead, if we can stay present and acknowledge what's really going on without judgment or self-criticism, we can act in more skillful ways. It's not about rolling over or giving up our values, but about seeing what's really there and allowing ourselves to make choices based on reality rather than a fantasy we hold about who our child should be.

It's called radical acceptance because it's a radical act to accept what's here, just as it is—and because it's extremely hard to do. Acknowledging our expectations and wishes about our kids and then seeing where our kids might not match our expectations can be painful. It's not giving up on our kids, but instead seeing them for who they really are and not trying to force them into being someone else. You can still be disappointed, sad, or fearful about your child, but you won't add to the pain by resisting what's in front of you. In the end, practicing radical acceptance can lead to a greater sense of calm over circumstances you likely can't influence anyway.

Let's apply this practice to a real-life scenario. Imagine you're the parent of a teenager who is disorganized and procrastinates. As the parent, you observe that this disorganization and tendency to wait until the last minute to get things done causes stress for your teen. (It certainly causes stress for you!) You know that if they could only get organized and plan ahead more, they'd be able to stay on top of their schoolwork and not always have a last-minute rush to get things done. And yet no matter how much you remind, nag, blame, criticize, and shame them (which most of us have done unwittingly in one form or another), they don't seem to change their ways. What if you changed yours? What if you decided to see your teen with compassion and kindness instead? What if you asked yourself, "Is this something they can change right now?" Maybe it is, maybe it isn't. When you look at the evidence, at all you've done to help them change—maybe you've bought them calendars and organizers, helped them create a filing system, or even arranged a teacher or tutor to regularly meet with them to go over their upcoming assignments—and then realize nothing has fundamentally changed, what then?

Okay, maybe this has helped them become a little more organized. But have you really changed them into an organized person? Probably not. However, you can see that they are a multifaceted person with many good qualities, even if "organized" and "planful" may not be some of them right now. You know that they're kind, funny, thoughtful, bright, and curious. Being organized or able to plan is only one facet of a person. They'll figure out their own systems and ways of organizing, because that's what is required of them by the world, not because you *will* it to be so. It turns out that the things they need to learn will eventually become important to them. They'll figure out ways to do them on their own as they experience the natural consequences of their behavior, not because you've explained it to them for the one-millionth time.

Knowing that you've supported your teen in being organized and planful, while accepting that they fundamentally may not be, can actually be liberating. You can let go of the burden of making them into something they're not right now; you can let them grow and develop into the young adult they're becoming at their own pace and on their own timeline.

EXERCISE: WORKING THROUGH RADICAL ACCEPTANCE

The following steps will help you work through some aspect of your child's behavior, character, appearance, temperament, or other quality that you don't like and that causes you suffering. This exercise may help you to see and cherish them as they are, not as you hope they might be.

Step 1: Write one thing about your teen/tween that disappoints you.

Step 2: What are your fears and judgments about this?

Step 3: List the constructive ways you've tried to shift this behavior or characteristic.

Step 4: Has what you've done helped change the behavior or characteristic? If so, how?

Step 5: Is there anything else you could do? If so, what?

_____

_____

_____

_____

_____

_____

_____

_____

Step 6: What would it look and feel like to accept that this might just be part of who your teen/tween is right now?

_____

_____

_____

_____

_____

_____

_____

_____

Step 7: In this moment, how might you let go of some of the responsibility you feel for what you can't control about your teen/tween?

_____

_____

_____

_____

_____

_____

_____

_____

Step 8: List some qualities of your teen/tween that you like, admire, and adore.

_____

_____

_____

_____

_____

_____

_____

_____

Step 9: What's available to you if you choose to see that your teen/tween is all these things at the same time?

_____

_____

_____

_____

_____

_____

_____

_____

Step 10: Fill in your teen's/tween's name in this statement:

I understand that _____ is a work in progress. I'm doing all I can to support _____'s growth. I'm letting go of what I can't control about _____, while staying engaged and committed to _____'s development. While doing this, I will honor my efforts and intentions as a parent and treat myself with gentleness and compassion.

SEPARATION MEDITATION

Start by getting comfortable in your chair. Once you have settled your body, begin paying attention to your breath. The purpose of breathing mindfully is to focus on each inhale and exhale in order to simply notice, accept, and be aware of your breath. Following your breath helps focus your attention and brings you into the present moment. When you attend to the breath itself, you allow thoughts and feelings to come and go without getting caught up in them.

Imagine there's a grounding cord that extends from the base of your spine down into the earth. What is it made of? Is it a root, a rope, a vine? Whatever it is, imagine it dropping down into the center of the earth, anchoring you and bringing you to the present moment. Now notice any pain or tightness or emotional discomfort in your body and imagine it flowing down through the grounding cord and into the earth. Let go of anything in your body that isn't serving you right now.

Now, with your eyes closed, imagine your teen is here standing in front of you. You are going to observe some basic facts that show how you are a different person from your teenager. To your teenager, you will imagine saying the following:

You are [age of teenager]. I am [my age].
I send your energy back to you. I take my
    energy back to me.

You are a student. I am a parent.

I send your energy back to you. I take my
   energy back to me.

You were born in [place teenager was born].
   I was born in [place you were born].
I send your energy back to you. I take my
   energy back to me.

Your hair is [description of teen's hair]. My
   hair is [description of your hair].
I send your energy back to you. I take my
   energy back to me.

You spend your day at school. I spend my
   day [in an office, at home, running
   around].
I send your energy back to you. I take my
   energy back to me.

You like to [activities your teen likes to do].
   I like to [activities you enjoy].
I send your energy back to you. I take my
   energy back to me.

We are two different people on two separate and distinct paths. I wish you
   well on your path. I wish myself well
   on mine.

*Now keep your eyes closed and return your focus
to your breathing and when you're ready, open your
eyes and return your focus to the room.*

If you would rather listen to a guided meditation, please visit https://mindfulparentingofteens.com/mindful-meditations/.

What was that Separation Meditation like for you?

_____

_____

_____

_____

_____

_____

_____

_____

_____

_____

_____

_____

_____

_____

_____

_____

Not everyone has the same experience doing this meditation. For some, this meditation brings up feelings of wistfulness or loss. Many of us are enmeshed in our kids' lives and can't imagine it any other way. There's something very tender about acknowledging that our children are unique beings on their own path, separate and distinct from ours. Others find it freeing to realize that their children are on their own journey and that as much as we love and support them, their lives will take their own course and they'll find their own way. You may not experience any of these thoughts or emotions, and that's okay too. We offer these meditations so you can experiment with them and find the ones that work for you.

CLOSING

When you let go of your expectations about your teen, what becomes available to you?

_____

_____

_____

_____

_____

_____

_____

_____

_____

_____

_____

_____

_____

_____

_____

_____

CHAPTER 7

The Power of Intentions: Parenting with Purpose

You could look at each [child] as a little Buddha or Zen master, your own private mindfulness teacher, parachuted into your life, whose presence and actions were guaranteed to push every button and challenge every belief and limit you had . . . These trials[of raising children] are not impediments to either parenting or mindfulness practice. They are the practice, if you can remember to see it this way.

—*Jon Kabat-Zinn,* Wherever You Go, There You Are: Mindfulness Meditation in Everyday Life

PONDER THIS

Find a baby or toddler photograph of your teen that captures their personality. What do you love about this photo?

_____

_____

_____

_____

_____

_____

_____

_____

_____

_____

_____

We start this chapter on the power of intentions by reminding you of what you love about your son or daughter. Keeping a baby or toddler photo somewhere you can see it every day is a good way to connect with your teen's endearing characteristics. What were they like when they were little? Affectionate, curious, exuberant, bashful, busy, independent, helpful? It's likely that your child's essential qualities as an adorable six-month-old are still there, buried underneath that awkward twelve-, fourteen-, or sixteen-year-old exterior. These qualities will reemerge as they get older, so keeping a baby photo nearby reminds us of the aspects of them that make them so precious to us. Keep breathing through the teen years and know that you'll be seeing this lovable person again.

PARENTING WITH PURPOSE

Part of mindful parenting is being conscious of our intentions and aware of how we want to be with our children. It can be challenging to parent with intention, in part because of the fast pace of modern life—for parents and teens alike. In our "always on" culture, we're faced with new input and information coming at us all the time, leading to our endless to-do lists and jam-packed schedules. As the pace accelerates, it's easy to find ourselves scrambling to keep up and simply reacting to the next demand coming our way. Mindfulness calls upon us to stop running on autopilot and to conduct our lives in a more purposeful way.

Being intentional means thinking and acting deliberately based on our priorities and values. Rather than responding reflexively, we make conscious decisions about how we want to be and where we want to direct our time and energy. Setting intentions takes thought. It starts by clarifying what's important to us and carefully weighing the things we care about. Our intentions create an overarching frame of reference that drives our smaller, day-to-day actions. When we're able to act with intention, we are more confident that we're living in alignment with our values.

In Buddhism, intentions are different from goals (which are also important). A goal suggests the achievement of a measurable result, while an intention is a principle to live by or a guiding light. An intention is a mindset you choose to embody *right now* without being attached to a specific outcome. Our intentions inform how we meet each moment, how we interpret the world around us, and how we make decisions. Parenting intentions might sound like this:

- I intend to be kind to my family members.
- I choose to be compassionate with my difficult child.
- I will show my teen unconditional love even when she's rebelling.
- I will speak to my kids in ways that don't cause harm.
- I will maintain my equanimity during the stormy teenage years.
- I'm grateful for the good things in my life and in my family.

As you think about setting intentions, you may want to start with the end in mind. Every time you set an intention, you are inclining your mind toward this desired end. If you imagine how you want things to be, you can then take actions that support that vision. Ask yourself the big questions like "How do I want to be as a parent?" "What kind of person do I want my teen to become?" "What values do I want to communicate to them?" These kinds of questions help you identify your intentions. The meditation at the end of this chapter guides you through this process. After the meditation, there's a place to write down what came up for you.

The benefit of setting intentions is that they provide us with a moment-to-moment road map for how we want to be as parents. Daily transition points can be a natural time to revisit intentions. For instance, when you get up in the morning, you might take a moment to think about how you want to meet the day. As you're on the way to pick up your child after school or on your way home from work, you might give some thought to how you'll greet your son or daughter after a long day for both of you. When you're turning in for the night, you might spend a few minutes letting go of any anger so you can wish them a good night of sleep. Creating these habits ends up driving our actions.

A final word on mindful parenting: be intentional about your expectations for this parenting phase in general. Do you expect these years to be fraught—or are you trying to experience them with an open mind and an open heart? A simple but powerful intention is to try to stay connected and maintain a loving relationship, even though your teen's developmental mission is to push you away. Yes, teens can be incredibly trying, but they can also be wildly creative, loving, witty, fun, and passionate. Can you set an intention to appreciate their engaging qualities (remember that cute baby pic!) amid the day-to-day challenges of being their parent?

HOW LIVING WITH INTENTION LOWERS STRESS

If you have butterflies in your stomach, ask them into your heart.

—*Cooper Edens,* If You're Afraid of the
Dark, Remember the Night Rainbow

Gaining clarity about your intentions and values can reduce some of the stress of parenting. Health psychologist Dr. Kelly McGonigal at Stanford University has studied stress for decades and has written a bestselling book on the subject. She defines stress this way: "Stress is what arises when something you care about is at stake."[1] Dr. McGonigal observes that stress and meaning are linked; we don't stress out about things that we don't care about. In fact, she argues that a happy life will include stress, because stress comes from doing things that create purpose and love. If you're doing something that's meaningful to you, at some point it's likely to challenge you. The feeling of stress is a signal that what you're undertaking is important—and parenting is by far one of the most important things we can ever do.

Interestingly, the more she studied the topic, the more Dr. McGonigal learned that what makes stress unhealthy is our *belief* that it's bad for us. After spending the first part of her career warning people of how dangerous stress was in and of itself, she discovered it's the combination of the stress and the *belief* that it's bad that causes the real harm to our health. People who experienced stress but didn't view it as entirely negative led healthier lives. The upshot of her work is that if we change our mindset and believe that at least some stress can be helpful, we are better able to cope with it.

In addition, Dr. McGonigal and her colleagues discovered a powerful mindset intervention to reduce stress. They conducted a study in which students were asked to write about their most important values and how their day-to-day activities related to those values. The researchers found that writing about values not only helped the subjects determine what was meaningful in their lives, but it provided context for why they did the things they did, and it reduced the stress associated with doing them. The students who wrote about their values felt more powerful, in control, and strong while also feeling more loving, connected, and empathetic toward others. An activity that was previously perceived as stressful or annoying was now perceived as a meaningful undertaking that supported the things they held most dear. For example, a student may have felt burdened that they had to care for a younger sibling, but when they put it in the context of how they valued the importance of family, they felt less stressed about doing it.

One fascinating part of this experiment was that it required only a ten-minute intervention. After a mere ten minutes of writing, the subjects experienced a perspective shift that endured years later when they were retested. And they benefited from these positive effects even if they couldn't recall having done the writing exercise in the first place!

EXERCISE: LIVING YOUR VALUES

Below, please write about a value that's important to you as a parent. What makes this value important to you? How do you live out this value in your daily life? You can write about something that feels meaningful and important right now or something you aspire to do. It could be a principle you already live by or one you want to make more important in your life. Identify the value and then spend ten minutes writing about it. You can start here, but you might want to grab your journal or additional paper if you plan to write for the full ten minutes, as recommended.

A value that's important to me as a parent is:

_____

Why is this value important to me? And how do I manifest (or could I manifest) this value in my day-to-day life as a parent?

_____
_____
_____
_____
_____
_____
_____
_____

Keep these reflections in mind the next time you feel stressed. To help you remember your value, you could create a physical reminder of it, like a bracelet with the word on it, a screen saver with a picture that represents that value, or a keychain that you carry all the time. Dr. McGonigal's research showed that people who had a physical reminder of what was meaningful to them dealt with adversity even better than those who only did the ten-minute writing exercise.

SETTING INTENTIONS MEDITATION

Start this meditation by getting comfortable in your chair. and letting all the tension and tightness in your body melt away.

Turn your attention to your breathing. Take a few moments in silence to take several long, slow, deep breaths, making sure that the exhale is as long as or longer than the inhale, because this will help calm your body and soothe your nervous system. Return your breathing to its normal pace, and continue to breathe in relaxation and breathe out tension.

As you allow yourself to sink into this relaxed state, take a moment to ask yourself some powerful questions. The answers to these questions will help clarify your intentions as a parent. The first question is: "What is present when I'm at my best as a parent?" Give yourself several moments in silence to contemplate this question. Observe the thoughts and emotions that arise when you ask yourself this question.

As you're breathing slowly and steadily, turn your attention to this next question: "What kind of relationship do I want with my teen?" Just take a moment or two to think about what kind of relationship you want to create with your child or children during the teen years. Allow whatever thoughts come up to rise to the surface of your awareness.

Now ask yourself, "What do I want to do more of as a parent?" Tune in to your intuition and listen for what comes up when you ask yourself the question.

Receive whatever insight emerges with curiosity and kindness.

Next, ask yourself, "What do I want to do less of as a parent?" Sit quietly and observe any thoughts or emotions that come up as you contemplate the question. Invite these thoughts without self-criticism or judgment.

Now ask yourself, "What gets in the way of being the parent I want to be?" Continue to breathe in and out and notice any thoughts or emotions that come up in response to this question. Notice if you find yourself judging them and let that judgment go. Instead, focus on any insight you might be receiving.

And finally, "What's one thing I could do this week that would move me closer to having the relationship I want with my teen?" Let your inner wisdom tell you what that one thing might be, and take a few still moments to create an intention about what you will do this week to make that one thing happen.

Turn your attention back to your body and your breath. Notice your body sitting comfortably in the chair and the steadiness of your breathing, as you gently inhale and exhale. Gradually become aware of the sounds in the room around you. And when you're ready, open your eyes and take a few minutes in silence to write down what came up during the meditation.

If you would rather listen to a guided meditation, please visit https://mindfulparentingofteens.com/mindful-meditations/.

Record here what came up in your meditation about intentions. What was that Setting Intentions Meditation like for you?

_____

_____

_____

_____

_____

_____

_____

_____

_____

_____

_____

_____

PONDER THIS

What is present when I'm at my best as a parent?

_____

_____

_____

_____

_____

What kind of relationship do I want with my teen?

_____

_____

_____

_____

_____

What do I want to do more of as a parent?

_____
_____
_____
_____
_____
_____

What do I want to do less of as a parent?

_____
_____
_____
_____
_____
_____

What gets in the way of being the parent I want to be?

_____
_____
_____
_____
_____
_____

What's one thing that I could do this week that would move me closer to having the relationship I want with my teen?

_____
_____
_____
_____
_____
_____

NOTE TO SELF

Using the answers to the questions you just answered, write yourself a letter with any words of wisdom that came to you during this meditation. Seal it, put it aside, and open it at a later date when you need some insight and encouragement.

PRACTICING GRATITUDE

We cannot be grateful without being thoughtful. We cannot shift our mental gears into neutral and maintain a grateful lifestyle. This is why gratitude requires contemplation and reflection.

—Robert A. Emmons, Thanks!: How the New
Science of Gratitude Can Make You Happier

No book on mindfulness would be complete without addressing the profound effects of gratitude. We cultivate gratitude as a show of appreciation for the things that we have and the things that we are. Gratitude is an intentional mindset that asks us to open our hearts and look for the many gifts we receive every day. Gratitude can give us a perspective on negative events that helps us recover from them more quickly.

In chapter 5, we talked about showing appreciation for our teens and acknowledging them when they behaved appropriately or did something right. Another way to be more grateful is to create the habit of deliberately meditating on, thinking about, or writing down the things we're grateful for. With practice, gratitude can become a way of life that's integrated into everything we do.

Psychology Professor Robert Emmons at the University of California, Davis, is the leading expert in the science of gratitude. He believes that gratitude consists of two parts.[2] The first is the "celebration of the good." When we're grateful, we affirm that there is good in the world. Not that our lives are perfect or that we don't face problems and pain, but that there are always good things around us if we look for them.

The second component of practicing gratitude is recognizing that good things come from outside of us. We humbly acknowledge and receive benefits from others, including people, animals, nature, or (depending on our beliefs) God or the universe.

The benefits of practicing gratitude are compelling. Over the last two decades, Dr. Emmons and his colleagues have studied thousands of people and have observed that those who have a regular gratitude practice have stronger immune systems and lower blood pressure. They also exercise more, sleep better, and are less bothered by aches and pains. In addition to these physical benefits, they also gain psychological benefits, including higher levels of positive emotions and more alertness, optimism, happiness, pleasure, and joy. And they experience social benefits: they are more helpful, generous, compassionate, forgiving, and outgoing, while feeling less lonely and isolated.[3] With a list like this, is there any reason why a person *wouldn't* practice gratitude?

For most of us, holding gratitude in our hearts takes practice—whether through a formal gratitude journal where we record the things we're thankful for on a regular basis, or more informally by reflecting on our blessings as we wake up in the morning or before going to sleep at night. These practices help us be more deliberate in focusing our attention on the good—and not taking these things for granted. It's important to pay attention to the good, because positive emotions don't last long. Research shows that we quickly habituate to a new positive development, and then our brains want to move to the next novel thing. Because of our brain's negativity bias, it takes longer to form a positive memory than to embed a negative one.[4] Recognizing when we are having a positive thought or emotion and then making a purposeful effort to prolong and sink into it can increase joyfulness. Gratitude brings us to and keeps us in the present—what are we thankful for in this moment?—so we can savor pleasurable experiences while they're happening and allow our brains to more thoroughly process and hardwire these happy memories.

GRATITUDE MEDITATION

Start this meditation by getting comfortable in your chair. Take a deep breath and let all the tension and tightness in your body melt away.

Focus your attention on your breathing. Take a long, slow, deep breath, in through the nose and out through the mouth. Drop into silence and continue taking long, slow, deep breaths, making sure that the exhale is as long as or longer than the inhale; this will help calm you and soothe your nervous system. Allow your body to breathe in relaxation and breathe out tension. .

Allow yourself to go deeper into a meditative state, and take a moment to be grateful for your body.

Reflect on how your body serves you every day: your limbs, muscles, skeleton, and inner organs, all perfectly designed to keep you healthy and functioning. What do you appreciate about your body?

Take a moment to notice what else in your life you're grateful for. Practicing gratitude on a regular basis can decrease stress and increase happiness and well-being. What if you were to express gratitude for everything in your life? Not just the good things, but also the things that seem bad or hard, because sometimes they are opportunities for us to grow and learn. Gratitude invites you to say a blessing for all things in your life.

Call to mind the people in your life for whom you're grateful. Bring your attention to all the people who positively impact you and support you. It might be your family, friends, coworkers, school or spiritual communities, a person who works in your local grocery store or delivers your mail, even your ancestors and elders. Think of all the people you're grateful for. Notice how this makes you feel.

Now bring to mind your teenager. What is it about your teen that you're grateful for? What qualities about them do you value and admire? Take a moment to reflect on how grateful you are that this person is in your life. Breathe into your gratitude and appreciation of your teen.

Now reflect on the resources you have available to you. Call to mind the material objects that make your life easier, more efficient, or more pleasant. What are the things that you appreciate and make you feel good? Take a few breaths to savor them.

Now let your mind explore the natural resources that you appreciate. The earth, the sky, the trees, the flowers, the animals ... whichever aspects of the natural world bring you pleasure and joy. Allow yourself to appreciate these things as you continue to breathe slowly and steadily.

Finally, let your mind wander to anything else that you're grateful for. Take a few quiet, still moments to call to mind anything else that brings you a sense of delight.

End this meditation by holding that feeling of gratitude. Let your heart be full of gratitude, joy, and appreciation. Observe what gratitude feels like in your body. Remember that you don't have to meditate to feel gratitude. You can simply check in with yourself throughout the day and notice the things around you that you appreciate.

And when you're ready, open your eyes and return your attention to the room.

PONDER THIS

Take a moment to list here some things you are grateful for.

_____

_____

_____

_____

_____

_____

MY WISH FOR YOU

I would maintain that thanks are the highest form of thought; and that gratitude is happiness doubled by wonder.

—*G. K. Chesterton,* A Short History of England

I am grateful to you for joining me in this journey to mindfully parent your teen. I want to end this book where I started, by acknowledging that you are already a mindful parent. The fact that you've read this book from beginning to end shows that you care deeply about your relationship with your teenager. It's likely that you are already parenting with compassion, courage, presence, and intention. I hope this book will be a reference that you can return to over and over, pulling its mindfulness tools out of your kit when you need them. These practices are intended to help us better manage ourselves, which is ultimately the only thing we really have control over as our children grow, develop, and become young adults. Keep practicing mindfulness so you can stay calm, clearheaded, and openhearted. You'll find that as you use these tools more and more, you'll experience less conflict and more loving moments with your teen. And after all, isn't that what we all want?
My parting wishes for you:

> *May you be happy,*
> *may you be healthy,*
> *may you be peaceful,*
> *may you live with ease.*
> *Blessings!*

CLOSING

What do you want to keep in mind as you parent mindfully and with purpose?

_____

_____

_____

_____

_____

_____

_____

_____

_____

_____

_____

_____

_____

_____

_____

APPENDIX: A MINDFUL PARENTING TOOLKIT

I need to . . .	Mindful exercise/tool
Learn how to meditate	See "Meditation in Practice" in chapter 2.
	Listen to the guided meditations at https://mindful parentingofteens.com/ mindful-meditations/
Respond more effectively in recurring conflicts	See "Mindful Thoughts, How Interpretations Drive Reactions" in chapter 3.
Identify my emotions and notice how my emotions impact my responses	See "Commonly Felt Emotions" and "Noticing Emotions Exercise" in chapter 4.

Disengage from an emerging conflict with my teen	See "Disengagement Strategies: Pause and Breathe, Talk Less, Stop Talking, Walk Away" in chapter 4.
Take care of myself	See "Taking Care of Yourself," "Self-Compassion Practice," and "Loving-Kindness Meditation" in chapter 4.
Say no to my teen	See "Saying No: A Four-Step Process, Broken Record, Last Word" in chapter 5.
Make a request of my teen	See "Making a Request: A Three-Step Process, Broken Record, Last Word" in chapter 5.
Recover after we have a conflict	See list of recovery tools in chapter 5.
Get my teen to open up to me	See "Mindful Listening: A Parent's Superpower" in chapter 5.
Accept what I can't change about my teen	See "Radical Acceptance" exercise in chapter 6.
Disentangle from my teen	See "Separation Meditation" in chapter 6.

Live with intention	See "Living Your Values" exercise in chapter 7.
Practice gratitude	See "Gratitude Meditation" in chapter 7.
Stop criticizing myself as a parent	See "Parenting Mantras Meditation" in chapter 5 and "Note to Self" in chapter 7.
Stay connected with my teen	See "Loving-Kindness Meditation" in chapter 4 and "Increase Positivity by Expressing Affection, Gratitude, and Kindness," in chapter 5 and "Setting Intentions Meditation" in chapter 7.

RESOURCES

MEDITATION RESOURCES

Research shows that meditating daily helps reduce stress and increase overall well-being. Follow this link to access parenting meditations that will help you in your daily practice: https://mindfulparentingofteens.com/mindful-meditations/.

BOOKS AND WEBSITES

There are many wonderful books about mindfulness, teenagers, and parenting teenagers. Here are some favorites to increase your knowledge and understanding.

Hanson, Rick, and Richard Mendius. *Buddha's Brain: The Practical Neuroscience of Happiness, Love, and Wisdom.* Oakland: New Harbinger Publications, 2009.

Jensen, Frances E. *The Teenage Brain: A Neuroscientist's Survival Guide to Raising Adolescents and Young Adults.* New York: HarperCollins Publishing, 2015.

Kabat-Zinn, Jon. *Wherever You Go, There You Are: Mindfulness Meditation in Everyday Life.* New York: Hachette, 2009.

Kastner, Laura, and Jennifer Wyatt. *The Launching Years: Strategies for Parenting from Senior Year to College Life.* New York: Clarkson Potter, 2002.

Lythcott-Haims, Julie. *How to Raise a Young Adult: Break Free of the Overparenting Trap and Prepare Your Kids for Success.* New York: Henry Holt and Company, 2015.

Mogel, Wendy. *The Blessing of a B Minus: Using Jewish Teachings to Raise Resilient Teenagers.* New York: Scribner, 2010.

Neff, Kristin, and Christopher Germer. *The Mindful Self-Compassion Workbook: A Proven Way to Accept Yourself, Build Inner Strength, and Thrive.* New York: Guilford Press, 2018.

Riera, Michael. *Staying Connected to Your Teenager: How to Keep Them Talking to You and How to Hear What They're Really Saying.* Boston: DeCapo Press, 2017.

Siegel, Daniel J. *Brainstorm: The Power and Purpose of the Teenage Brain.* New York: Jeremy P. Tarcher/Penguin, 2013.

Stanford Children's Health. "The Growing Child: Adolescent (13 to 18 Years)." Last accessed June 19, 2019. https://www .stanfordchildrens.org/en/topic/default?id=the-growing -child-adolescent-13-to-18-years-90-P02175.

Wolf, Anthony E. *I'd Listen to My Parents If They'd Just Shut Up: What to Say and Not Say When Parenting Teens.* New York: HarperCollins, 2011.

NOTES

CHAPTER 1

1. "Major Depression: Prevalence of Major Depressive Episode among Adolescents," National Institute of Mental Health, last modified February 2019, https://www.nimh.nih.gov/health/statistics/major -depression.shtml#part_155031.
2. Anthony E. Wolf, *I'd Listen to My Parents If They'd Just Shut Up:What to Say and Not Say When Parenting Teens* (New York: HarperCollins, 2011), 1–9, 53–56.
3. Kristin A. Moore, Lina Guzman, Elizabeth Hair, Laura Lippman, and Sarah Garret, "Parent-Teen Relationships and Interactions: Far More Positive Than Not," *Child Trends Research Brief*, #2004-25 (December 2004), 1–2.
4. John W. Santrock, *Life-Span Development*, 11th ed. (New York: McGraw-Hill, 2008), 386–438.
5. Louann Brizendine, *The Female Brain* (New York: Morgan Road Books, 2006), 38.
6. Brizendine, 38–39.
7. Daniel J. Siegel, *Brainstorm: The Power and Purpose of the Teenage Brain* (New York: Jeremy P. Tarcher/Penguin, 2013), 67.
8. Richard A. Miech, Lloyd D. Johnston, Patrick M. O'Malley, Jerald G. Bachman, John E. Schulenberg, and Megan E. Patrick, *Monitoring the Future National Survey Results on Drug Use, 1975–2018, Volume 1: Secondary School Students* (Ann Arbor: University of Michigan Institute for Social Research, 2019): 15, http://www.monitoring thefuture.org/pubs/monographs/mtf-vol1_2018.pdf.
9. Miech et al., 10-11.

10. Elizabeth Witwer, Rachel K. Jones, and Laura Lindberg, *Sexual Behavior and Contraceptive and Condom Use among US High School Students, 2013–2017* (New York: Guttmacher Institute, 2018), 4–5, https://www.guttmacher.org/report/sexual-behavior-contraceptive-condom-use-us-high-school-students-2013-2017.

11. Caitlin Abar and Robert Turrisi, "How Important Are Parents during the College Years?: A Longitudinal Perspective of Indirect Influences Parents Yield on Their College Teens' Alcohol Use," *Addictive Behaviors* 33, no. 10 (October 2008): 1360–61, https://doi.org/10.1016/j.addbeh.2008.06.010.

12. Sara B. Johnson, Robert W. Blum, and Jay N. Giedd, "Adolescent Maturity and the Brain: The Promise and Pitfalls of Neuroscience Research in Adolescent Health Policy," *Journal of Adolescent Health* 45, no. 3 (September 2009): 216–22, https://www.ncbi.nlm.nih.gov/pmc/articles/PMC2892678.

13. Frances E. Jensen and Amy Ellis Nutt, *The Teenage Brain: A Neuroscientist's Survival Guide to Raising Adolescents and Young Adults* (New York: HarperCollins, 2015), 36–37, 40.

14. Rick Hanson and Richard Mendius, *Buddha's Brain: The Practical Neuroscience of Happiness, Love, and Wisdom* (Oakland: New Harbinger Publications, 2009), 68.

15. Daniel J. Siegel and Tina Payne Bryson, *The Whole-Brain Child: 12 Revolutionary Strategies to Nurture Your Child's Developing Mind* (New York: Delacorte Press, 2011), chap. 3.

16. Siegel and Bryson, chap. 3.

17. Daniel Goleman, *Emotional Intelligence: Why It Can Matter More Than IQ* (New York: Bantam Books, 1995), 17–20.

18. Siegel, *Brainstorm*, 106.

19. Siegel, 80.

20. Carol S. Dweck, *Mindset: The New Psychology of Success* (New York: Random House, 2016), 6–11.

CHAPTER 2

1. Jon Kabat-Zinn, *Wherever You Go, There You Are: Mindfulness Meditation in Everyday Life* (New York: Hachette, 2009), 4.

2. Daniel Goleman and Richard J. Davidson, *Altered Traits: Science Reveals How Meditation Changes Your Mind, Brain, and Body* (New York: Avery, 2017), 98.

3. Goleman and Davidson, *Altered Traits*, 10.

4. Goleman and Davidson, *Altered Traits*, 81–82.

5. Madhav Goyal, Sonal Singh, Erica M. S. Sibinga, et al., "Meditation Programs for Psychological Stress and Well-Being: A Systematic Review and Meta-Analysis," *JAMA Internal Medicine* 174, no. 3 (March 2014): 357–68, http://dx.doi.org/10.1001/jamainternmed.2013.13018.

6. Rick Hanson and Richard Mendius, *Buddha's Brain: The Practical Neuroscience of Happiness, Love, and Wisdom* (Oakland: New Harbinger Publications, 2009), 81–82.
7. Goleman and Davidson, *Altered Traits*, 74.

CHAPTER 4

1. Matthew D. Lieberman, Naomi I. Eisenberger, Molly J. Crockett, Sabrina M. Tom, Jennifer H. Pfeifer, and Baldwin M. Way, "Putting Feelings into Words: Affect Labeling Disrupts Amygdala Activity in Response to Affective Stimuli," *Psychological Science* 18, no. 5 (May 2007): 421–28, https://doi.org/10.1111/j.1467-9280.2007.01916.x.
2. Rick Hanson and Richard Mendius, *Buddha's Brain: The Practical Neuroscience of Happiness, Love and Wisdom* (Oakland: New Harbinger Publications, 2009), 49–52.
3. Anthony E. Wolf, *I'd Listen to My Parents If They'd Just Shut Up: What to Say and Not Say When Parenting Teens* (New York: HarperCollins, 2011), 31–33.
4. Wolf, 57–59 .
5. Kristin Neff and Christopher Germer, *The Mindful Self-Compassion Workbook: A Proven Way to Accept Yourself, Build Inner Strength, and Thrive* (New York: Guilford Press, 2018), 31.
6. Neff and Germer, 34–36.
7. Neff and Germer, 25.

CHAPTER 5

1. Anthony E. Wolf, *I'd Listen to My Parents If They'd Just Shut Up: What to Say and Not Say When Parenting Teens* (New York: HarperCollins, 2011), 62–64.
2. Wendy Mogel, *The Blessing of a B Minus: Using Jewish Teachings to Raise Resilient Teenagers* (New York: Scribner, 2010), 37.
3. Wolf, *I'd Listen to My Parents If They'd Just Shut Up*, 93–95.
4. Jim Loehr and Tony Schwartz, *The Power of Full Engagement: Managing Energy, Not Time, Is the Key to High Performance and Personal Renewal* (New York: Free Press, 2003), 32–34.
5. Barbara L. Fredrickson, *Positivity: Top-Notch Research Reveals the 3-to-1 Ratio That Will Change Your Life* (New York: Three Rivers Press, 2009),32, 36.
6. Mogel, *The Blessing of a B Minus*, 46.
7. Wolf, *I'd Listen to My Parents If They'd Just Shut Up*, 102–6.
8. Lee Rowland and Oliver Curry, "A Range of Kindness Activities Boosts Happiness," *Journal of Social Psychology* 159, no. 3 (2019): 340–43.

CHAPTER 7

1. Kelly McGonigal, *The Upside of Stress: Why Stress Is Good for You and How to Get Good At It* (New York: Avery, 2015), xi–xii, 68–75.
2. Robert A. Emmons, *Thanks!: How Practicing Gratitude Can Make You Happier* (New York: Houghton Mifflin, 2008), 4.
3. Emmons, 30–35.
4. R. Baumeister, E. Bratlavasky, C. Finkenaur, and K. Vohs, 2001. "Bad is Stronger than Good," Review of General Psychology 5: 323–70

ACKNOWLEDGMENTS

I've always said this book practically wrote itself. That's because my business partner, Ann Arora, MFT, and I researched and designed the curriculum for our Mindful Parenting of Teens workshop, then led it together for years. We added material here, edited it there, and incorporated suggestions from the many thoughtful parents who took our class. The book was just a matter of writing it down. Although Ann was not able to complete the book with me due to other professional commitments, she was very involved in the early stages of writing and development. I'm grateful to Ann for her incomparable insight, intelligence, and sense of humor. I couldn't have asked for a better collaborator.

I also want to thank the many parents who showed up at our workshops to learn and share their experiences parenting teenagers. Somehow all the back talk and attitude is easier to bear when you know you're not the only one going through it. There is power in sticking together, and I want to acknowledge the courage and compassion of our workshop participants. You know who you are.

❦ I'm grateful to the inspiring teachers who have shared their wisdom with me and many fortunate others: Marc Lesser, Lori Schwanbeck, Sura Kim, Heather Glidden, Chela Harper, Rita O'Malley, Jaime Lindauer, Megan Pryor Lorentz, Jaqueline Aaron, and Joy Libby. The world is a better place because of you.

Many thanks to the crackerjack team at Girl Friday Productions: Sara Addicott, production editor; Ingrid Emerick, developmental editor; Georgie Hockett, brand marketing manager; Christina Henry de Tessan, strategic partnerships; Kathleen Lynch, cover designer; Rachel Marek, book designer; Meredith Jacobson, copyeditor; and Jenn Zaczek, proofreader. They are a smart, savvy crew that consistently brought their best to this endeavor. Their expertise and skills were invaluable from beginning to end.

I also want to appreciate the trusted friends who took the time to read all or parts of this material—with special thanks to Patty LaDuke for her astute yet gentle editing. How lucky am I to have amazing girlfriends and family members who've provided years of support and advice (mostly while walking): Deidre, Winn, Claire, Lori O., Laurie O., Patty K., Meredith, Karen H., Jane E., Chapin, Gretchen, Nancy, Tamara, Laura, Jane C., Diane, Cora, Janie R., Kate F., Lori B., Shelly, Joy, Cynthia, Jacqueline, MarySue, Karen R., Helena, Faith, SI Moms 10, SHB class of 2013 moms, WPO Forummates, Kristin, Ellen, Kathy, Gigi, and countless others who've helped me maintain my equilibrium.

And of course, to my dear family: deep appreciation to my husband, Bill, and my three children who (when they're not driving me crazy) make being a wife and mother a joy. I can always trust you guys to provide a "feedback-rich environment" with love, wit, and generosity. I adore each of you.

ABOUT THE AUTHOR

Photo © Elizabeth Burkett

Wynn Burkett is a certified executive coach and leadership consultant who has been coaching individuals and teams and facilitating workshops for nearly twenty years. She is a long-time student of mindfulness and has completed a yearlong meditation teacher training through the Sura Center, as well as Search Inside Yourself Leadership Institute's Engage program, which was developed at Google to bring mindfulness to individuals, groups, and communities. With psychotherapist Ann Arora, MFT, she created the workshop How to Tame

Your Teen by Taming Yourself First: A Mindfulness-Based Approach to Parenting, which she has led for seven years. The workshop provides education and tools to help parents stay calm and connected to their teens during the challenging adolescent years. Most importantly, she's a parent of three and enjoys teaching this subject because it reminds her to be a more mindful parent herself. She has a BA from Stanford University and an MBA from the Yale School of Management.

Made in the USA
Lexington, KY
30 October 2019